WITHDRAWN FROM LIBRARY

MODERN ESSAYS AND SKETCHES

A. A. MILNE

From a pen-drawing by E. Heber
Thompson, after a photograph by
"Coster—Photographer of Men"

MODERN ESSAYS AND SKETCHES

Edited by

J. W. MARRIOTT

Essay Index Reprint Series

BOOKS FOR LIBRARIES PRESS
FREEPORT, NEW YORK

R68-00989

PR
1367
m 35

1968

First Published 1935
Reprinted 1968

LIBRARY OF CONGRESS CATALOG CARD NUMBER:
68-22928
PRINTED IN THE UNITED STATES OF AMERICA

ACKNOWLEDGMENTS

FOR permission to use copyright material thanks are due
and are hereby tendered to :
  Mr. James Agate for " A Word to the Amateurs " ;
Mr. Oswald Barron for " Nine Lives " from *Day In and
Day Out* ; Miss Sylva Norman for " Secrecy and Eve-
lina " ; Mr. James Bone for " The Matrix of London " ;
Mr. Harold Brighouse and the *Manchester Guardian* for
" Dukes' Excursions " ; Mr. Ivor Brown and the *Man-
chester Guardian* for " Farewell to the Fair " ; Mr. Val
Gielgud for " Radio Drama " from *The Times Broad-
casting Number*, 1934 ; Miss Winifred Holtby for " Other
People's Lives " ; Mr. H. M. Tomlinson and Messrs.
Cassell and Co., Ltd., for " A Midnight Voyage " from
London River ; Miss Rosalind Vallance for " Washing
Day." Messrs. Jonathan Cape, Ltd., for " The Greatest
Test Match " from *Days in the Sun*, by Neville Cardus,
and " The Beauty of Shadow " from *Poems and the
Spring of Joy*, by Mary Webb ; Messrs. Cassell and Co.,
Ltd., and Miss Storm Jameson for " Student Days "
from *No Time like the Present* ; Messrs. Chatto and
Windus, and Mr. Norman Douglas for " Rome " from
Alone ; Messrs. R. Cobden-Sanderson, Ltd., for " The
Tragic Years " from *Little Innocents* by E. M. Delafield ;
Messrs. Hodder and Stoughton, Ltd., and Major Beith
for " The Seven Ages " from *The Shallow End* ; Messrs.
John Lane, the Bodley Head, Ltd., for " The Achieve-
ment of the Cat " from *The Square Egg*, by Saki (H. H.
Munro) ; Messrs. Longmans, Green, and Co., Ltd., and
Mr. Edmund Blunden for " To Twelfth Night " (January
Pictures) from *The Face of England* ; Messrs. Methuen
and Co., Ltd., for " A Piece of Chalk " from *Tremendous
Trifles*, by G. K. Chesterton ; Messrs. Methuen and Co.,
Ltd., and the authors for " On Them " from *On Nothing*,
by Hilaire Belloc, " The Lord of Life " from *The More I*

ACKNOWLEDGMENTS

See of Men, by E. V. Lucas, " Witches and Whatnot "
from *This Other Eden*, by E. V. Knox, " Cats " from *The
Pleasures of Ignorance*, by Robert Lynd, "The Charm of
Golf " from *Not That It Matters*, by A. A. Milne, and
"Photographs" from *Apes and Angels*, by J. B. Priestley;
Messrs. James B. Pinker and Son for " Joys of the
Street " by the late C. E. Montague ; and The Times
Publishing Co., Ltd., for " The Legend of Buffalo Bill "
from *The Times Literary Supplement*, October, 1929.
Acknowledgment is also due to Mr. Max Beerbohm for
" The Fire," taken from *Yet Again*, published by Messrs.
Chapman and Hall.

CONTENTS

CONTENTS

INTRODUCTION

THE word " essay " was first used by Montaigne in the sixteenth century to describe a form of literature in which he excelled, but it must not be assumed, as is often done, that Montaigne invented the essay itself. The critic of to-day is sceptical about sudden creations. Historical research has taught him to look for a gradual evolution from obscure beginnings. The essayist is born and not made, but the essay, like Topsy, " just growed."

A literary form which continues to flourish after hundreds of years obviously has a vitality of its own ; equally obviously it has sufficient flexibility to adapt itself to frequent changes of environment. The essay has as many shapes as Proteus, and for this reason a precise definition is difficult if not altogether impossible. Sir John Squire recently described it as polymorphous, and a glance through any typical collection will justify the epithet. One may find in it a treatise or a thesis written with scientific detachment, a random (probably facetious) commentary on some topic of the hour, or even a character sketch which breaks into dialogue and almost becomes a short story. Professor J. B. S. Haldane's dissertation on the causes of war, Macaulay's lengthy study of Lord Clive, Addison's portrait of Sir Roger de Coverley, and Lamb's story of the accidental discovery of roast pork are all liable to appear in a collection of essays.

The genuine essay is a kind of disquisition handled in a light-hearted and personal manner. It deals in a cursory way with a subject as it affects the writer. That is to say, the subject is both reflected from and refracted through the temperament of the author, and vice versa. Any person of average ability, and the run of a reference library, can write a treatise, but the writer of genius can write an essay on the most trivial theme, and make it amusing and significant. An essay on a pin lying in the road, remarks Mr. Robert Lynd, may light up some square inch of human nature.

When a scientist writes about the skylark, for example, we learn much about the bird and nothing about the scientist; but if Mr. G. K. Chesterton wrote about the skylark we should probably learn a little about the bird and a great deal about Mr. Chesterton. To illustrate this point the editor has included four treatments of the same subject in the present volume.

The essay is a severe test of a writer, and has been described as the Ulysses' bow of literature. At the same time it is a delightful medium for expression. The prejudice which so many adults feel against the essay is due to its early association with home work and examinations. This is particularly unfortunate, because it is based upon a delusion. The majority of so-called essays are not essays but treatises. " The Foreign Policy of Queen Elizabeth," and " The Influence of

Transport upon Commerce " are not essay subjects at all.

The essays in this collection are modern and
therefore representative of the post-war world.
Elderly readers may dislike them—many of them
will—but it cannot be helped. The man who
objects to modern novels, modern plays, and
modern journalism, also objects no less em-
phatically to modern architecture, modern sculp-
ture, and modern dress. These things are all of
a piece. As the familiar platitude has it, every
form of art reflects the age which produces it.

What are the characteristic features of our own
day ? The list (which must appear a trifle in-
congruous) must include aeroplanes, streamline
motors, ferro-concrete buildings, service flats,
arterial roads, jazz bands, fox-trots, crooners,
super-cinemas, cocktails, wireless, flood-lighting,
the democratization of " pleasure," the habit of
" thinking in headlines," and a sense of frustra-
tion due to our inability to keep pace with the
swiftness of mechanical invention and social
science. There are many more, but these will
suffice.

Now it is probably absurd to argue that crazy
pavements and steel furniture have a direct
influence upon the literary work of the present
day ; but it may not be altogether ridiculous
to contend that the modern spirit manifests itself
in a thousand forms. Eighteenth-century literature was static, like its life ; it paraded itself,
like its fashionable people ; it was ostentatious,
like its houses and furniture. The nineteenth
century became dynamic, preferring movement
to elegance, and we see indisputable evidences

in its poetry and its politics, in its melodrama and its machines. Twentieth-century literature, expressing the twentieth-century mind, is inextricably entangled with the spirit which finds satisfaction in syncopated music, transatlantic flights, and the creations of Elstree and Hollywood.

The old-time writer cared little about speed. He was tempted to pose, to attitudinize, to " show himself " like Mr. Turveydrop, to indulge in digression and leisurely moralizing ; but the modern writer must get on and come to immediate grips with his subject. We praise his economy of words, his deliberate sacrifice of ornament, his dislike for rhetoric. His style is lean, sinewy, athletic. He has rid himself of superfluous verbiage as he has cleared his flat of foolish ornaments and gaudy wallpaper. The modern journalist is on the speed-track ; the modern dramatist employs a sort of streamlining in his play ; the modern speaker takes the short cuts and " gets there " in the minimum of time.

We still enjoy the leisurely essays of Goldsmith and Hazlitt, but the idiom is that of another age, and has the interest of Chippendale or Sheraton furniture. The modern essayist is incisive and " right pithy." Until a few years ago the writer handled his subject in a dignified manner, propounding, elaborating, constructing, and finishing (as it were) with a gesture. He had a respect for form which is fast disappearing, and the essays of the youngest writers are often little more than sketches and improvisations on a given theme. The older writers betray their impatience with the new order ; the feeling of revolt, though it may not be expressed, runs as an undercurrent in their thought ; they still cherish the traditional ideals, and look forward with misgiving. The younger writers, occasionally irreverent and often casual, give the impression that they are groping their way. They are not sure of themselves. The whole collection reveals the moods of an age of experiment and transition.

But perhaps the greatest difference between the old essay and the new lies not so much in literary craftsmanship as in the attitude of mind and general philosophy from which it springs. One cannot dogmatize about the change which has come about without stirring up controversy, but to the present writer it seems that the modern mind is more flexible and resilient than the old. We are no longer content to accept rigid rules of conduct, for example, but prefer to judge by referring to vital principles. We want to know exactly why a pronouncement is made, and whether one has the right to adjudicate at all. We have less reverence for authority, and none for pomposity. It might be said that the modern world is more Greek and less Roman in its outlook, that it is more feminine than masculine, that it appreciates the curve more than the straight line. To the man of fixed ideas it appears that the modern world is becoming lax in its morals, and departing from strict standards of truthfulness and discipline. But this criticism may be due to misunderstanding. His position reminds us of the old grammarian who mourns because a living language declines to keep the rules of a dead language ; or of the old logician who laments the loss of Euclid in a world of electrical engineering.

A Roman road looks straight when seen on a map or from the sky, but actually it moves up hill and down dale like a switchback. A river appears to wander without any definite purpose, yet it consistently follows a natural law, and seen from another angle it may look straight enough. The point of view makes all the difference. The pre-war man thinks the youth of to-day is lacking in the traditional virtues of strength and consistency; the young people accuse their elders of acting by rule-of-thumb, and murmur sarcastically about the laws of the Medes and Persians. Old ideas, like old nations, had rigid boundaries; but we live in the days of aviation and relativity.

The old essayist was inclined to dictate and to assert his authority. He expected his readers to accept his judgment. But the modern world has a fierce dislike for the man who tries to impose his will upon others. It objects to the tyranny of the Victorian father, whose rhetorical fireworks neither dazzle nor impress the post-war generation. The essayist of to-day does not lecture nor preach; he offers suggestions, expounds ideas, makes tentative speculations. He writes with the air of a man who says " This is what I think about things. You may agree or not. Please yourself ! "

Lord Bacon wrote his essays for publication in volume form, but few essayists have worked with such a motive. Addison, Steele, Johnson, Goldsmith, Stevenson, and a hundred others did their best work in writing for the papers of their day. If they were living now they would adapt themselves to the requirements of the modern editor, and a vastly greater circle of readers. Some of the longest essays would be " boiled down " to make Third Leaders for the *Times,* or back page articles for the *Manchester Guardian.*

The essayist of to-day chooses his own subject, but he generally finds some " topical peg " on which to hang his thoughts and to give them " news value." He often deals with a trivial theme, or a matter of fugitive interest, but if he is a true essayist he will say something of permanent significance, and will contrive to say it in a way which is memorable.

J. W. M.

MODERN ESSAYS AND SKETCHES

THE LEGEND OF BUFFALO BILL

The Times Literary Supplement

THE process by which heroes are manufactured for the exhilaration of the public has attracted little serious investigation, except perhaps in Hohenzollern Prussia. It is, none the less, an art neither accidental nor capricious in its selective technique. Where the historian strives—so far as frailty of records and human prejudice will allow—to reveal what actually happened, it is left to the novelist, like the bard of old, to submit a symbol instead of a survey, or launch a legend instead of a liturgy. The method sounds facile enough, but is actually governed by rigid conventions. Popular approval may be stormed along the romantic byways of social distinction, personal beauty, supreme physical prowess, or picturesque misfortune, and should the background be equally amiable, the making of a hero is merely a matter of presentation. But there are still the proprieties. It is, very naturally, usual and even proper that these human legends of history should not only illustrate a period, and thus give it dramatic expression, but that they should be separated by the kindly veil of time from their literary impresarios. To the historian the last rising of the Jacobites presents an insignificant military campaign, whereas to the novelist and poet, and consequently the entire reading public, it has provided in Prince Charlie a supreme hero completely equipped with beauty, youth, courage, a lost crown, and superb misfortune. The episode demanded imaginative consolidation, and by the genius of Sir Walter Scott the romantic (and also commercial) future of the Highlands was assured. In a similar way the eclipse of the highwayman through the invention of steam necessitated the legend of the turnpike ; and Harrison Ainsworth, adopting the miserable and obscure footpad, Dick Turpin, set him riding to York, and in doing so rang up the curtain upon that exhilarating myth, the Duval of the cross-roads. But the point to remember is that in each case the hero was dead.

What would seem incredible would be that a novelist could select a living character, and having endowed him with all the qualities of a superman, set him loose to symbolize the popular notions of an historical background. And yet that was exactly what happened to Buffalo Bill. In his discovery, his carefully established reputation, and his place in the estimation and affection of the world, the career of William Cody is quite without precedent, and in these days of instantaneous corroboration may never be repeated. Circumstances peculiar to his generation gave such a supreme piece of effrontery a sporting chance, which his own exuberant character proceeded to mould into a solid achievement.

To examine the social conditions of America between 1830 and 1880 is to realize the inevitability of " Buffalo Bill." In 1830 the Eastern States were consolidated into a civilization remote from the fierce pioneering days of the eighteenth century, and mildly tickled by the dim memories of the extinct forest Indian in the sturdy novels of Fenimore Cooper. It had become a kind of national creed that over the Missouri River lay a trackless wilderness, where the Indian Territory had stabilized the problem of the Redskin, and where the buffalo roamed over an arid desert without value for settlement or agriculture. Transport remained the key to the wilderness ; and though the trader plied his wares with the plains Indians and the trapper damped his fire in the lonely corries of the Rockies, the conquest of the West was not yet within reach. After 1830 successive events, reacting one upon another without organized intention, but creating new conditions with immense rapidity, converted the convictions of a century. Pressure from increasing emigration gave heart to pioneers to push off in ever longer wagon trains to Santa Fé and Oregon. The time is coming when these argonauts of the plains will take their just place in the story of the West. They have too long provided a playground for the novelist. Their records paint a landscape, not of whooping Indians, but of intense solitude and monotony. In a time when historical research is delivering one shrewd blow after another at the frontier of the dime novel, it is not without importance to study in an excellent Western magazine, the *Frontier*, the unvarnished personal records of those who set out to discover land or gold, and frequently found only an unmarked grave. Their printed narratives are a saga of the press of civilization westward. But it was not the saga for that particular age, which craved for something more thrilling than making history behind an ox wagon. The old West had come and gone within a few years, and the Eastern States, restless and eager for distraction after the Civil War, demanded a closer acquaintance with those last desperate days.

There were, however, problems not easily overcome. The background must be picturesque and triumphant, the sentiments noble and courageous, the qualities and appearance of the living symbol attractive and convincing. To " Ned Buntline," that remarkable American novelist, whose works of fiction are as many as those of Scott and Dickens, the chance was golden. He decided to bring the West to the East. But where it is child's play to impress a reader in print, or an audience on the screen, it is little short of magic to give them a hero of actual flesh and blood. That was Buntline's genius. He discovered in a young man called William Cody the virtues of flexibility and temperament which could emulate without conscious hypocrisy the superhuman qualifications of Buffalo Bill. In the personal biographies and autobiographies of Cody—all of which were written long after his fame was assured—every care is exercised to belittle Buntline and to suggest that he persuaded his hero to leave the plains because of his unequalled reputation as a frontiersman and Indian fighter. It is therefore essential to examine the career of Cody before he became established as the nightmare of the Redskin, the foe of the bandit, and the rescuer of innumerable maidens in distress. Take, for example, Mr. Zane Grey's apotheosis of him in *The Last of the Great Scouts*. " He was symbolical of the heroic West. He inspired the pioneer, guided the soldier, and helped the builders of the railroad." It is time such extravagance was moderated. These are but sounding words. Mr. Grey must be well aware that Cody was not a great scout, that if the pioneers of his day were inspired by anything it was for virgin soil or rumours of gold, that the final hunting down of desperate bands of Indians was an undertaking best unchronicled, and that the calling of butcher is (and was to Cody) more a commonplace of our human necessities than a passionate dream of Empire.

A candid and moderate work has recently appeared in America entitled *The Making of Buffalo Bill—A Study in Heroics*. Mr. Walsh has written it with the assistance of Jimmy Baker, who worshipped Cody, and the son of Nate Salsbury, who made the Wild West show. It is well informed and moderate ; a study in heroics, but also a study in heroism. It is not possible any longer to blind our eyes to the tinsel in Buffalo Bill, but it is henceforth within our power to continue our old allegiance to William Cody. Mr. Walsh has analysed with admirable impartiality the claims of the man upon whom the unscrupulous gaze of Buntline rested. He was not a famous scout and frontiersman like Jim Bridger, or a notorious gunman like Wild Bill Hickok, or a professional Indian fighter like Frank North. It was not upon the plains, but only in the fiction of Buntline that Buffalo Bill became the " boy Indian slayer," the killer of the McCandless gang, the dreaded foe of the Redskin, the bright star of the Civil War, and the distinguished Chief of Scouts upon whom the American frontier force depended. The authentic facts of his life are not so dazzling. He was born in Iowa in 1846, was a herder when he was eleven, probably spent a short time with the pony express, that hazardous service which, for a few years, preceded the railroad conveying mails across the wilderness, acted as a hospital orderly during most of his connection with the Union forces, did not meet Custer until 1867, and left the plains for good at the age of twenty-six. It is more than probable that he served with the Fifth Cavalry on some scouting expeditions ; and long after his spurious fame there is first-hand evidence he killed Yellow Hand, the Red Indian Chief, in a single-handed encounter. But his career holds no place in frontier records, or in the index of Major Ganoe's *History of the United States Army* ; and his killing of buffalo was no more exceptional than that of all the other Buffalo Bills and Neds with whom the great plains swarmed in an era when thirty-one million of these distracted animals were ruthlessly slaughtered for their hides, or for the amusement of wealthy American and English sportsmen.

Buntline was not disturbed. He knew what the East expected, and taking out his pen dashed off his first Buffalo Bill story. It was read by Cody with the utmost amazement. It " told of deeds he had never done and could never hope to match, of talents which he did not possess, and noble sentiments which he did not boast." He was a simple young man in 1869, and he might well gasp, " Gosh, what things they write ! " But having excited public interest, Buntline must let the East see Buffalo Bill ; and accordingly wrote with his customary speed a lively drama called *The Scouts of the Prairie*, in which the author appeared himself (which was fortunate, as he alone knew the words), and hired ten bogus Indian warriors from the street to be killed in two performances daily. The critics had heard the play had taken four hours to write, and expressed their surprise. But it gave Cody a vision of the future. He knew well enough that the plains afforded no longer the casual employment of his youth. He was married, and had already failed as hotel keeper, in real estate, and as a freighter. But he was disappointed with the result of the theatrical venture. He thought Buntline—who had discovered him asleep under a wagon at Summit Springs—should have done better.

It was the old story of dropping the pilot. Buntline went out and John Burke came in, and remained in for forty-four years. Burke was the supreme Press agent. He may, as his enemies said, have had " nothing but brass and wind as a stock in trade," but he had also an enduring loyalty and adoration for Cody. With the Buffalo Bill novels revealing new achievements weekly, and the papers accumulating and amending, and always strengthening the legend, Burke was indefatigable in juggling with half-truths. The Western myth was everything. Cody had been a civilian guide to Carr—he was therefore a

scout, and being a scout must be Chief of all
Scouts and take the rank and pay of colonel.
Burke even grew his hair long and appeared
himself as " Arizona John," surely an indication
in a citizen of Columbia of an excellent humour.
Bill Hickok of Abilene joined them for a season,
but was too authentic of the real West. Having
lost his temper and quenched the spot light with
a bullet, he requested the stage carpenter to " tell
that long-haired son-of-a-gun I have no more use
for him or his damned show business."

But all the novels in the world, and all the
amazing clap-trap of Burke would not have kept
Cody from financial embarrassment and consequent eclipse had not the third great engineer
of his destiny appeared in Nate Salsbury. Cody
was a wretched business man. It was therefore
a memorable day when, in 1882, he listened in a
Brooklyn restaurant to Salsbury conceiving and
detailing the future pageant of the West, with
its real Indians, and bronchos, and Texan cowboys, the buffalo, and Deadwood coach. Cody
was a quick mover. He had not realized that
Salsbury was as much the show as " Buffalo Bill."
So he went into partnership with Dr. W. F.
Carver, who was running a Western show as *The
Evil Spirit of the Plains*. Carver was a dentist
by profession, and had " sunk a lead mine trying
to learn to shoot." He wore long hair, and was
a gifted liar. But as a business man he was on
Cody's level. Burke could get the publicity ;
Cody could win the crowd ; the rest was chaos.
Shortly afterwards Cody placed himself in the
skilful charge of Salsbury. It was a partnership
which made his fortune. The great show was no

longer a dream, or even a speculation. To the Eastern States and finally to Europe came a huge and competent presentation of the West as it had become familiar to the public. Genuine cowboys, in all the regalia of the rodeo, strengthened the belief that the life of the cattleman was one long round of shooting up bars, and conquering mustangs ; genuine Sioux Indians, fresh from the latest rising, were beaten twice daily in accordance with the tradition of the white man's unconquerable valour and superior marksmanship. There was Sitting Bull, that ancient diehard, and Annie Oakley, whom he called " Little Sure Shot," and old John Nelson, with his Indian wife and half-caste papooses. There was Captain Bogardus, and Pawnee Bill, and a host of others. But above all, transcending all, riding into the arena—an unforgettable figure—was Buffalo Bill himself. By virtue of its originality, its real quality, and its profound appeal to the youth of the world, its genius of business management, and its Press advertisement, the Wild West Show was bound to " make Barnum look to his laurels."

It was with this final development that Cody signed his fabulous adventure tales himself. It gave them the final touch of incontestable truth. Sometimes, before his decline and necessitous struggles, he shrank from the incessant execution of Red Indians, a race which had proved their superiority as fighting men throughout three centuries of methodical extermination by vastly superior numbers.

" I am sorry," he wrote to his publishers, " to have to lie so outrageously in this yarn. My hero has killed more Indians on one war trail than I have killed in all my life. But I understand this is what is expected in border tales. If you think the revolver or bowie knife are used too freely, you may cut out a fatal shot or stab, wherever you deem it wise."

The great project of conquering Europe fired John Burke. But it was essential that the British public should believe that Buffalo Bill was really " the goods." Even to-day the older generation recall Cody more as a great showman than an authenticated scout. It is only since the wide circulation of stories and " Lives " that the British boy, who never saw the circus, reverences Buffalo Bill as the intrepid Western fighter. Burke knew the value of personal achievements. There was accordingly a whip-round among the elderly and good-natured generals under whom Cody had served. But even retired generals could not elevate him from the position of a civilian guide. So the State of Nebraska obliged by making him a colonel of the National Guard. The title of " Honourable " he had long cultivated in deference to an invitation (which he did not accept) to stand for the Nebraska Legislature. Supported by the friendly, though guarded, testimonies of the generals, and billed as " The Hon. Colonel William Cody," he impressed the sceptical British public. Readers of that excellent book, *Seventy Years a Showman*, by " Lord " George Sanger, will recall the amusing rivalry of the two great exhibitions when Cody landed in England. For some time the British public had become so attached to the Wild West stories that Sanger ran " Scenes from Buffalo Bill," with two real buffaloes, a few unreal Indians, some mules, and a bogus coach. Cody set about stopping this in the Law Courts. After the contest, which he lost, Sanger decided to steal a march on the American invasion, and became a lord in his own right, and so remained. It was a title taken no less lightly than some, and providing considerably more amusement than most.

There is no question that Buffalo Bill conquered Europe. Queen Victoria bowed to the Stars and Stripes as Cody rode past her box. Quite carried away, she ordered a command performance for the royal guests who had come to the Jubilee. They made a party of three hundred, and after that the show was on its feet for fifteen years. Buffalo Bill was the lion of the London season. What was the explanation ? James Russell Lowell wrote sourly : " I think the true key to this eagerness for lions—even of the poodle sort —is the dullness of the average English mind." The analysis of General Sherman was nearer the mark : " You have caught one epoch of this country's history, and have illustrated it in the very heart of the modern world." Buntline had seen it coming, and gave it expression in his novel ; Salsbury brought the American frontier into the heart of London. Burke paused at nothing that would add to Cody's prestige. But it was Buffalo Bill himself, magnificent, debonair, the perfect centaur, who made the show. He was the hero of a hundred tales. So were his Indians. So was the Deadwood coach. Who that saw it will ever forget that rumbling piece

of wreckage with its hordes of whooping braves !
And yet we must once more steel our hearts to
withstand another shock. Mr. Walsh remarks :

" The first stagecoach into Deadwood was
driven by Richard Clark—known in the dime
novels as ' Deadwood Dick.' An inquisitive
visitor, during the fiftieth anniversary celebration
in 1926 found Deadwood Dick still there, and
asked him : ' How many men did you kill ?
How many stage hold-ups were you in ? How
many times did Indians attack your party and
scalp all but you ? How many times was your
life saved only by the swiftness of your horse or
the sureness of your trusty weapon ? ' Deadwood
Dick listened patiently, and then replied : ' Not
one,' and to complete the disillusionment he added
impressively, ' I tell the truth.' "

The European tour was little short of a triumph.
It paused to enable Cody to rush across America
to the Sioux outbreak of 1890, which provided
him with a fresh advertisement, relit the flame of
Indian savageries as a practical accessory in
advertisement and tales, and handed over to him
a batch of unhappy " hostiles " as wards in his
next departure for England. The show developed
from a purely Western background into an ex-
hibition of horsemanship by the " Rough Riders
of the World." Since Indian hostilities were over,
campaigns in Cuba, South Africa, and China were
drawn upon. Perhaps no more pathetic instance
of the fall in Redskin stock could be given than
the period when Indians were disguised as Chinese
warriors !

The inevitable decline set in with the retirement, through illness, of Salsbury, in 1895. It was a fatal loss. A Chicago critic had already remarked :

" Cody's nonsensical posings grow more enticing every year. A trifle more obese, he bowed, pranced, and cavorted . . . a charming bundle of airs and nonsense. Meanwhile a little man who couldn't break a glass ball with an axe, will maintain his watchful patrol around ticket offices and main entrances, and nobody will know that the big amusement doings inside are of his creating and planning more than any one else. His name is Nate Salsbury. . . ."

There was now only Burke left, and Burke could not go on beating the big drum unless the people walked up. He did his best. In 1897 he assured the public that " they were not travelling to make money, sir, but only to do good." To Cody the future was becoming a little ominous. " I grow," he said, " very tired of this sort of sham hero-worship." From thence onwards, and principally to get out of the arena, he invested several fortunes in mines and property, and lost them all.

Later on, to his despairing appeal, Salsbury, now nearing the end, replied with his habitual courage and good sense : " We cannot regulate the universe, and we must get along with as little friction and worry as possible if we care to stay on earth much longer." These strange, brooding words were little consolation to Cody. Whether he cared to or not, his natural courage forbade surrender. Salsbury died, and the substance had finally departed from the show, leaving only the shadow. From 1902 to Cody's collapse and death in 1917, there followed a succession of fare-wells, growing ever feebler — farewells to the public, to prosperity, to any hope of restful old age, and, finally, to life itself. In that last period the picture of Buffalo Bill and his faithful hench-man, Burke—both now old and broken—is suf-ficiently tragic, and also sufficiently heroic. Separated from his wife, stricken with grief at the death of his daughter Arta, loaded with debt, he struggled on with another Continental tour. His new partner, Bailey, died in 1906, and Cody came home to open once more in New York. He was now hopelessly insolvent. What was worse, the decline was obvious. Finally, the Wild West was closed by the sheriff and sold up for a song. His famous horse was knocked down to a loyal bidder from Nebraska. But with indomitable courage the old man remarked, " I have to start life over again with no capital." For a moment there came a turn for the better. Reconciled to his wife, Cody organized the Red Indian action of Wounded Knee for the movies. He bought a typewriter and sat down to reel off his auto-biography. With the declaration of the European War he planned to revive the old military interest of the show. But all he could get was a place in some one else's circus. As Mr. Walsh has justly commented, " No dime novelist or Press agent ever invented for Buffalo Bill a more courageous act than this—that in his seventy-first year he took up his rifle again, mounted his horse, and shot the glass balls." He was near his end, but he never faltered.

" Many a day that autumn they thought he was going to come to the end that he dreaded—death in the arena. Behind the great curtains they helped him into the saddle. He sat there, slumped down, waiting his cue. But when Baker snapped out, " Ready, Colonel ? " he could jerk himself erect, shoulders back, head up. In the noble pose that moulded him to his horse he rode out to face his audience as gaily as ever, to lead the march, to shoot the glass balls, to flourish his sombrero in parting salute. Still holding the pose, he reined his horse backward through the parted curtains, the centaur still. But as the curtains swung between him and the crowd, he fell forward in the saddle with a groan, and Baker would be there to catch him and help him to the ground. Day after day it happened so. He held out to the last."

The life was finished, but the legend remained. Ned Buntline, who moulded it, wrote two hundred novels, and is forgotten ; Nate Salsbury, who gave it stability, lived and died behind the curtain ; unconscionable John Burke, who worshipped Cody for over forty years, has taken his place in the shadows. Only Buffalo Bill remains.

To the older generation his name recalls rather wistful memories of a hard seat in a crowded circus, suddenly frozen to stillness, as that unforgettable figure, cantering into the arena, rode into their hearts and there remained. Looking backward, our honest inclination is to denounce the purely accurate analysis. There is in crude truth something arid and suffocating. Contemporary history becomes more and more insistent that in the prolonged conflict with Nature and the Indian there was little of romance or heroics. And yet the spirit of imagination is full of betrayals. It is now over a decade since Cody died, but the place where he lies on the steep summit of Lookout Mountain promises to become something more vital than a showman's tomb. It may even—for want of another—stand as a symbol of the intrepid spirit which, during three centuries, pierced the impenetrable forests to the Mississippi, braved the frontiers of the Missouri, and, crossing the great plains, united the American people from East to West.

A PIECE OF CHALK

G. K. Chesterton

I REMEMBER one splendid morning, all blue and silver, in the summer holidays, when I reluctantly tore myself away from the task of doing nothing in particular, and put on a hat of some sort and picked up a walking-stick, and put six very bright coloured chalks in my pocket. I then went into the kitchen (which, along with the rest of the house, belonged to a very square and sensible old woman in a Sussex village), and asked the owner and occupant of the kitchen if she had any brown paper. She had a great deal ; in fact, she had too much ; and she mistook the purpose and the rationale of the existence of brown paper. She seemed to have an idea that if a person wanted brown paper he must be wanting to tie up parcels ; which was the last thing I wanted to do ; indeed, it is a thing which I have found to be beyond my mental capacity. Hence she dwelt very much on the varying qualities of toughness and endurance in the material. I explained to her that I only wanted to draw pictures on it, and that I did not want them to endure in the least ; and that from my point of view, therefore, it was a question not of tough consistency, but of responsive surface, a thing comparatively irrelevant in a parcel. When she understood that I wanted to draw she offered to overwhelm me with note-paper, apparently supposing that I did my notes and correspondence on old brown paper wrappers from motives of economy.

I then tried to explain the rather delicate logical shade, that I not only liked brown paper, but liked the quality of brownness in paper, just as I liked the quality of brownness in October woods, or in beer, or in the peat-streams of the North. Brown paper represents the primal twilight of the first toil of creation, and with a bright-coloured chalk or two you can pick out points of fire in it, sparks of gold, and blood-red, and sea-green, like the first fierce stars that sprang out of divine darkness. All this I said (in an off-hand way) to the old woman ; and I put the brown paper in my pocket along with the chalks, and possibly other things. I suppose every one must have reflected how primeval and how poetical are the things that one carries in one's pocket ; the pocket-knife, for instance, the type of all human tools, the infant of the sword. Once I planned to write a book of poems entirely about the things in my pocket. But I found it would be too long ; and the age of the great epics is past.

.   .   .   .   .   .

With my stick and my knife, my chalks and my brown paper, I went out on to the great Downs. I crawled across those colossal contours that express the best quality of England, because they are at the same time soft and strong. The smoothness of them has the same meaning as the smoothness of great cart-horses, or the smoothness of the beech tree ; it declares in the teeth of our timid and cruel theories that the mighty are merciful. As my eye swept the landscape, the landscape was as kindly as any of its cottages, but for power it was like an earthquake. The villages in the immense valley were safe, one could see, for centuries ; yet the lifting of the whole land was like the lifting of one enormous wave to wash them all away.

I crossed one swell of living turf after another, looking for a place to sit down and draw. Do not, for heaven's sake, imagine I was going to sketch from Nature. I was going to draw devils and seraphim, and blind old gods that men worshipped before the dawn of right, and saints in robes of angry crimson, and seas of strange green, and all the sacred or monstrous symbols that look so well in bright colours on brown paper. They are much better worth drawing than Nature ; also they are much easier to draw. When a cow came slouching by in the field next to me, a mere artist might have drawn it ; but I always get wrong in the hind legs of quadrupeds. So I drew the soul of the cow ; which I saw there plainly walking before me in the sunlight ; and the soul was all purple and silver, and had seven horns and the mystery that belongs to all the beasts. But though I could not with a crayon get the best out of the landscape, it does not follow that the landscape was not getting the best out of me. And this, I think, is the mistake that people make about the old poets who lived before Wordsworth, and were supposed not to care very much about Nature because they did not describe it much.

They preferred writing about great men to

writing about great hills ; but they sat on the great hills to write it. They gave out much less about Nature, but they drank in, perhaps, much more. They painted the white robes of their holy virgins with the blinding snow, at which they had stared all day. They blazoned the shields of their paladins with the purple and gold of many heraldic sunsets. The greenness of a thousand green leaves clustered into the live green figure of Robin Hood. The blueness of a score of forgotten skies became the blue robes of the Virgin. The inspiration went in like sunbeams and came out like Apollo.

    .   .   .   .   .   .

But as I sat scrawling these silly figures on the brown paper, it began to dawn on me, to my great disgust, that I had left one chalk, and that a most exquisite and essential chalk, behind. I searched all my pockets, but I could not find any white chalk. Now, those who are acquainted with all the philosophy (nay, religion) which is typified in the art of drawing on brown paper, know that white is positive and essential. I cannot avoid remarking here upon a moral significance. One of the wise and awful truths which this brown-paper art reveals, is this, that white is a colour. It is not a mere absence of colour ; it is a shining and affirmative thing, as fierce as red, as definite as black. When (so to speak) your pencil grows red-hot, it draws roses ; when it grows white-hot, it draws stars. And one of the two or three defiant verities of the best religious morality, of real Christianity, for example, is exactly this same thing ; the chief assertion of religious morality is that white is a colour.

Virtue is not the absence of vices or the avoidance of moral dangers ; virtue is a vivid and separate thing, like pain or a particular smell. Mercy does not mean not being cruel or sparing people revenge or punishment ; it means a plain and positive thing like the sun, which one has either seen or not seen. Chastity does not mean abstention from sexual wrong ; it means something flaming, like Joan of Arc. In a word, God paints in many colours ; but He never paints so gorgeously—I had almost said so gaudily—as when He paints in white. In a sense our age has realized this fact, and expressed it in our sullen costume. For if it were really true that white was a blank and colourless thing, negative and non-committal, then white would be used instead of black and grey for the funeral dress of this pessimistic period. We should see City gentlemen in frock coats of spotless silver satin, with top hats as white as wonderful arum lilies. Which is not the case.

Meanwhile, I could not find my chalk.

 .   .   .   .   .   .

I sat on the hill in a sort of despair. There was no town nearer than Chichester, at which it was even remotely probable that there would be such a thing as an artist's colourman. And yet, without white, my absurd little pictures would be as pointless as the world would be if there were no good people in it. I stared stupidly round, racking my brain for expedients. Then I suddenly stood up and roared with laughter, again and again, so that the cows stared at me and called a committee. Imagine a man in the Sahara regretting that he had no sand for his hour-glass. Imagine a gentleman in mid-ocean wishing that he had brought some salt water with him for his chemical experiments. I was sitting on an immense warehouse of white chalk. The landscape was made entirely out of white chalk. White chalk was piled mere miles until it met the sky. I stooped and broke a piece off the rock I sat on : it did not mark so well as the shop chalks do ; but it gave the effect. And I stood there in a trance of pleasure, realizing that this Southern England is not only a grand peninsula, and a tradition and a civilization ; it is something even more admirable. It is a piece of chalk.

THE FIRE

Max Beerbohm

IF I were " seeing over " a house, and found in every room an iron cage let into the wall, and were told by the caretaker that these cages were for me to keep lions in, I think I should open my eyes rather wide. Yet nothing seems to me more natural than a fire in the grate.

Doubtless, when I began to walk, one of my first excursions was to the fender, that I might gaze more nearly at the live thing roaring and raging behind it ; and I daresay I dimly wondered by what blessed dispensation this creature was allowed in a domain so peaceful as my nursery. I do not think I ever needed to be warned against scaling the fender. I knew by instinct that the creature within it was dangerous —fiercer still than the cat which had once strayed into the room and scratched me for my advances. As I grew older, I ceased to wonder at the creature's presence, and learned to call it " the fire " quite lightly. There are so many queer things in the world that we have no time to go on wondering at the queerness of the things we see habitually. It is not that these things are in themselves less queer than they at first seemed to us. It is that our vision of them has been dimmed. We are lucky when, by some chance, we see again, for a fleeting moment, this thing or that as we saw it when it first came within our ken. We are in the habit of saying that " first impressions are best," and that we must approach every question " with an open mind " ; but we shirk the logical conclusion that we were wiser in our infancy than we are now. " Make yourself even as a little child," we often say, but recommending the process on moral rather than on intellectual grounds, and inwardly preening ourselves all the while on having " put away childish things," as though clarity of vision were not one of them.

I look around the room I am writing in—a pleasant room, and my own, yet how irresponsive, how snug and lifeless ! The pattern of the wallpaper blamelessly repeats itself from wainscot to cornice ; and the pictures are immobile and changeless within their glazed frames—faint, flat mimicries of life. The chairs and tables are just as their carpenter fashioned them, and stand with stiff obedience just where they have been posted. On one side of the room, encased in coverings of cloth and leather, are myriads of words, which to some people, but not to me, are a fair substitute for human company. All around me, in fact, are the products of modern civilization. But in the whole room there are but three things living : myself, my dog, and the fire in the grate. And of these lives the third is very much the most intensely vivid. My dog is descended, doubtless, from prehistoric wolves ; but you could hardly decipher his pedigree on his mild, domesticated face. My dog is as tame as his master (in whose veins flows the blood of the old cave men). But time has not tamed fire. Fire is as wild a thing as when Prometheus snatched it from the empyrean. Fire in my grate is as fierce and terrible a thing as when it was lit by my ancestors, night after night, at the mouths of their caves, to scare away the ancestors of my dog. And my dog regards it with the old wonder and misgiving. Even in his sleep he opens ever and again one eye to see that we are in no danger. And the fire glowers and roars through its bars at him with the scorn that a wild beast must needs have for a tame one. " You are free," it rages, " and yet you do not spring at that man's throat and tear him limb from limb, and make a meal of him ! " And, gazing at me, it licks its red lips ; and I, laughing good-humouredly, rise and give the monster a shovelful of its proper food, which it leaps at and noisily devours.

Fire is the only one of the elements that inspires awe. We breathe air, tread earth, bathe in water. Fire alone we approach with deference. And it is the only one of the elements that is always alert, always good to watch. We do not see the air we breathe—except sometimes in London, and who shall say that the sight is pleasant ? We do not see the earth revolving ; and the trees and other vegetables that are put forth by it come up so slowly that there is no fun in watching them. One is apt to lose patience with the good earth, and to hanker after a sight of those multitudinous fires whereover it is, after all, but a thin and comparatively recent crust. Water, when we get it in the form of a river, is pleasant to watch for a minute or so, after which period the regularity of its movement becomes as tedious as stagnation. It is only a whole seaful of water that can rival fire in variety and in loveliness. But even the spectacle of sea at its very best—say in an Atlantic storm—is less thrilling than the spectacle of one building ablaze. And for the rest, the sea has its hours of dullness and monotony, even when it is not wholly calm. Whereas in the grate even a quite little fire never ceases to be amusing and inspiring, until you let it out. As much fire as would correspond with a handful of earth or a tumblerful of water is yet a joy to the eyes, and a lively suggestion of grandeur. The other elements, even as presented in huge samples, impress us as less august than fire. Fire alone, according to the legend, was brought down from Heaven ; the rest were here from the dim outset. When we call a thing earthy, we impute cloddishness ; by " watery " we imply insipidness ; " airy " is for something trivial. " Fiery " has always a noble significance. It denotes such things as faith, courage, genius. Earth lies heavy, and air is void, and water flows down ; but flames aspire, flying back towards the heaven they came from. They typify for us the spirit of man, as apart from aught that is gross in him. They are the symbol of purity, of triumph over corruption. Water, air, earth, can all harbour corruption ; but where flames are, or have been, there is innocence. Our love of fire comes partly, doubtless, from our natural love of destruction for destruction's sake. Fire is savage, and so, even after all these centuries, are we, at heart. Our civilization is but as the aforesaid crust that encloses the old planetary flames. To destroy is still the strongest instinct of our nature. Nature is still " red in tooth and claw," though she has begun to make fine flourishes with toothbrush and nail-scissors. Even the mild dog on my hearthrug has been known to behave like a wolf to his own species. Scratch his master, and you will find the caveman. But the scratch must be a sharp one ; I am thickly veneered. Outwardly, I am as gentle as you, gentle reader. And one reason for our delight in fire is that there is no humbug about flames ; they are frankly, primevally savage. But this is not, I am glad to say, the sole reason. We have a sense of good and evil. I do not pretend that it carries us very far. It is but the toothbrush and nail-scissors that we flourish. Our innate instincts, not this acquired sense, are what the world really hinges on. But this acquired sense is an integral part of our minds. And we revere fire because we have come to regard it as especially the foe of evil—as a means for destroying weeds, not flowers ; a destroyer of wicked cities, not of good ones.

The idea of hell, as inculcated in the books given to me when I was a child, never really frightened me at all. I conceived the possibility of a hell in which were eternal flames to destroy every one who had not been good. But a hell whose flames were eternally impotent to destroy these people, a hell where evil was to go on writhing yet thriving for ever and ever, seemed to me, even at that age, too patently absurd to be appalling. Nor indeed do I think that to the more credulous children in England can the idea of eternal burning have ever been quite so forbidding as their nurses meant it to be. Credulity is but a form of incaution. I, as I have said, never had any wish to play with fire ; but most English children are strongly attracted, and are much less afraid of fire than of the dark. Eternal darkness, with a biting east wind, were to the English fancy a far more fearful prospect than eternal flames. The notion of these flames arose in Italy, where heat is no luxury, and shadows are lurked in, and breezes prayed for. In England the sun, even at its strongest, is a weak vessel. True, we grumble whenever its radiance is a trifle less watery than usual. But that is precisely because we are a people whose nature the sun has not mellowed—a dour people, like all northerners, ever ready to make the worst of things. Inwardly, we love the sun, and long for it to come nearer to us, and to come more often. And it is partly because this craving is unsatisfied that we cower so fondly over our open hearths. Our fires are makeshifts for sunshine. Autumn after autumn, " we see the swallows gathering in the sky, and in the osier-isle we hear their noise," and our hearts sink. Happy, selfish little birds, gathering so lightly to fly whither we cannot follow you, will you not, this once, forego the lands of your desire ? " Shall not the grief of the old time follow ? " Do winter with us this once ! We will strew all England, every morning, with bread crumbs for you, will you but try and help us to play at summer ! But the delicate, cruel rogues pay no heed to us, skimming sharplier than ever in pursuit of gnats, as the hour draws near for their long flight over gnatless seas.

Only one swallow have I ever known to relent.
It had built its nest under the eaves of a cottage
that belonged to a friend of mine, a man who
loved birds. He had a power of making birds
trust him. They would come at his call, circling
round him, perching on his shoulders, eating from
his hand. One of the swallows would come too,
from his nest under the eaves. As the summer
wore on he grew quite tame ; and when summer
waned, and the other swallows flew away, this
one lingered, day after day, fluttering dubiously
over the threshold of the cottage. Presently, as
the air grew chilly, he built a new nest for himself
under the mantelpiece in my friend's study.
And every morning, so soon as the fire burned
brightly, he would flutter down to perch on the
fender and bask in the light and warmth of the
coals. But after a few weeks he began to ail ;
possibly because the study was a small one, and
he could not get in it the exercise that he needed ;
more probably because of the draughts. My
friend's wife, who was very clever with her
needle, made for the swallow a little jacket of
red flannel, and sought to divert his mind by
teaching him to perform a few simple tricks. For
a while he seemed to regain his spirits. But
presently he moped more than ever, crouching
nearer than ever to the fire, and, sidelong, blinking dim, weak reproaches at his disappointed
master and mistress. One swallow, as the adage
truly says, does not make a summer. So this
one's mistress hurriedly made for him a little
overcoat of sealskin, wearing which, in a muffled
cage, he was personally conducted by his master
straight through to Sicily. There he was nursed

back to health, and liberated on a sunny plain. He never returned to his English home ; but the nest he built under the mantelpiece is still preserved in case he should come at last.

When the sun's rays slant down upon your grate, then the fire blanches and blenches, cowers, crumbles, and collapses. It cannot compete with its archetype. It cannot suffice a sun-steeped swallow, or ripen a plum, or parch the carpet. Yet, in its modest way, it is to your room what the sun is to the world ; and where, during the greater part of the year, would you be without it ? I do not wonder that the poor, when they have to choose between fuel and food, choose fuel. Food nourishes the body ; but fuel, warming the body, warms the soul too. I do not wonder that the hearth has been regarded from time immemorial as the centre, and used as the symbol, of the home. I like the social tradition that we must not poke a fire in a friend's drawing-room unless our friendship dates back full seven years. It rests evidently, this tradition, on the sentiment that a fire is a thing sacred to the members of the household in which it burns. I daresay the fender has a meaning as well as a use, and is as the rail round an altar. In *A Modern Utopia* these hearths will all have been rased, of course, as demoralizing relics of an age when people went in for privacy and were not always thinking exclusively about the State. Such heat as may be needed to prevent us from catching colds (whereby our vitality would be lowered, and our usefulness to the State impaired) will be supplied through hot-water pipes (white enamelled), the supply being strictly regu-

lated from the municipal water works. Or has
Mr. Wells arranged that the sun shall always be
shining on us ? I have mislaid my copy of the
book. Anyhow, fires and hearths will have to
go. Let us make the most of them while we
may.

Personally, though I appreciate the radiance
of a family fire, I give preference to a fire that
burns for myself alone. And dearest of all to
me is a fire that burns thus in the house of
another. I find an inalienable magic in my
bedroom fire when I am staying with friends ;
and it is at bedtime that the spell is strongest.
" Good-night," says my host, shaking my hand
warmly on the threshold ; " you've everything
you want ? " " Everything," I assure him ;
" good-night." " Good-night." " Good-night,"
and I close my door, close my eyes, heave a long
sigh, open my eyes, set down the candle, draw
the armchair close to the fire (my fire), sink down,
and am at peace, with nothing to mar my happiness except the feeling that it is too good to be
true.

At such moments I never see in my fire any
likeness to a wild beast. It roars me as gently
as a sucking dove, and is as kind and cordial
as my host and hostess and the other people in
the house. And yet I do not have to say anything to it, I do not have to make myself agreeable to it. It lavishes its warmth on me, asking
nothing in return. For fifteen mortal hours or
so, with few and brief intervals, I have been
making myself agreeable, saying the right thing,
asking the apt question, exhibiting the proper
shade of mild or acute surprise, smiling the

appropriate smile, or laughing just so long and just so loud as the occasion seemed to demand. If I were naturally a brilliant and copious talker, I suppose that to stay in another's house would be no strain on me. I should be able to impose myself on my host and hostess and their guests without any effort, and at the end of the day retire quite unfatigued, pleasantly flushed with the effect of my own magnetism. Alas, there is no question of my imposing myself. I can repay hospitality only by strict attention to the humble, arduous process of making myself agreeable. When I go up to dress for dinner, I have always a strong impulse to go to bed and sleep off my fatigue ; and it is only by exerting all my will-power that I can array myself for the final labours : to wit, making myself agreeable to some man or woman for a minute or two before dinner, to two women during dinner, to men after dinner, then again to women in the drawing-room, and then once more to men in the smoking-room. It is a dog's life. But one has to have suffered before one gets the full savour out of joy. And I do not grumble at the price I have to pay for the sensation of basking, at length, in solitude and the glow of my own fireside.

Too tired to undress, too tired to think, I am more than content to watch the noble and ever-changing pageant of the fire. The finest part of this spectacle is surely when the flames sink, and gradually the red-gold caverns are revealed —gorgeous, mysterious, with inmost recesses of white heat. It is often thus that my fire welcomes me when the long day's task is done. After I have gazed long into its depths, I close

32

my eyes to rest them, opening them again, with a start, whenever a coal shifts its place, or some belated little tongue of flame spurts forth with a hiss. Vaguely I liken myself to the watchman one sees by night in London, whenever a road is up, huddled half-awake in his tiny cabin of wood, with a cresset of live coal before him. . . . I have come down in the world, and am a night-watchman, and I find the life as pleasant as I had always thought it must be, except when I let the fire out, and awake shivering. . . . Shivering I awake, in the twilight of dawn. Ashes, white and grey, some rusty cinders, a crag or so of coal, are all that is left over from last night's splendour. Grey is the lawn beneath my window, and little ghosts of rabbits are nibbling and hobbling there. But anon the east will be red, and, ere I wake, the sky will be blue, and the grass quite green again, and my fire will have arisen from its ashes, a cackling and comfortable phœnix.

A MIDNIGHT VOYAGE

H. M. Tomlinson

OUR voyage was to begin at midnight from near Limehouse Hole. The hour and the place have been less promising in the beginning of many a strange adventure. Where the voyage would end could not be said, except that it would be in Bugsby's Reach, and at some time or other. It was now ten o'clock, getting towards sailing time, and the way to the foreshore was unlighted and devious. Yet it was somewhere near. This area of still and empty night railed off from the glare of the Commercial Road would be Limehouse Church. It is foolish to suppose you know the Tower Hamlets because you have seen them by day. They change. They are like those uncanny folk of the fables. At night, wonderfully, they become something else, take another form which has never been more than glimpsed, and another character, so fabulous and secret that it will support the tales of the wildest romanticist, who rightly feels that if such yarns were told of 'Frisco or Timbuctoo they might get found out. Was this the church? Three Chinamen were disputing by its gate. Perhaps they were in disagreement as to where the church would be in daylight.

At a corner where the broad, main channel of

electric light ended, and perplexity began, a policeman stood, and directed me into chaos. " Anywhere," he explained, " anywhere down there will do." I saw a narrow alley in the darkness, which has one gas lamp and many cobbled stones. At the bottom of the lane were three iron posts. Beyond the posts a bracket lamp showed a brick wall, and in the wall was an arch so full of gloom that it seemed impassable, except to a steady draught of cold air that might have been the midnight itself entering Limehouse from its own place. At the far end of that opening in the wall was nothing. I stood on an invisible wooden platform and looked into nothing with no belief that a voyage could begin from there. Before me then should have been the Thames, at the top of the flood tide. It was not seen. There was only a black void dividing some clusters of brilliant but remote and diminished lights. There were odd stars which detached themselves from the fixed clusters, and moved in the void, sounding the profundity of the chasm beneath them with lines of trembling fire. Such a wandering comet drifted near where I stood on the verge of nothing, and then it was plain that its trail of quivering light did not sound, but floated and undulated on a travelling road—that chasm before me was black because it was filled with fluid night. Night, I discovered suddenly, was an irresistible movement. It was swift and heavy. It was unconfined. It was welling higher to douse our feeble glims and to founder London, built of shadows on its boundary. It moved with frightful quietness. It seemed confident of its power. It swirled and eddied by the

35

piles of the wharf, and there it found a voice, though that was muffled ; yet now and then it broke into levity for a moment, as at some shrouded and alien jest.

There were sounds which reached me at last from the opposite shore, faint with distance and terror. The warning from an unseen steamer going out was as if a soul, crossing this Styx, now knew all. There is no London on the Thames, after sundown. Most of us know very little of the River by day. It might then be no more native to our capital than the Orientals who stand under the Limehouse gas lamps at night. It surprises us. We turn and look at it from our seat in a tram, and watch a barge going down on the ebb—it luckily misses the piers of Blackfriars Bridge—as if a door had unexpectedly opened on a mystery, revealing another world in London, and another sort of life than ours. It is as uncanny as if we had sensed another dimension of space. The tram gets among the buildings again, and we are reassured by the confined and arid life we know. But what a light and width had that surprising world where we saw a barge drifting as leisurely as though the narrow limits which we call reality were there unknown !

But after dark there is not only no River, when you stand where by day is its foreshore ; there is no London. Then, looking out from Limehouse, you might be the only surviving memory of a city that has vanished. You might be solitary among the unsubstantial shades, for about you are only comets passing through space, and inscrutable shapes ; your neighbours are Cassiopeia and the Great Bear.

36

But where was our barge, the *Lizzie*? I became aware abruptly of the skipper of this ship for our midnight voyage among the stars. He had his coat collar raised. The *Lizzie*, he said, was now free of the mud, and he was going to push off. Sitting on a bollard, and pulling out his tobacco pouch, he said he hadn't had her out before. Sorry he'd got to do it now. She was a bitch. She bucked her other man overboard three days ago. They hadn't found him yet. They found her down by Gallion's Reach. Jack Jones was the other chap. Old Rarzo they called him. Took more than a little to give him that colour. But he was All Right. They were going to give a benefit concert for his wife and kids. Jack's brother was going to sing ; good as Harry Lauder, he is.

Below us a swirl of water broke into mirth, instantly suppressed. We could see the *Lizzie* now. The ripples slipped round her to the tune of they-'avn't-found-'im yet, they-'avn't-found-'im-yet-they-'avn't. The skipper and crew rose, fumbling at his feet for a rope. There did not seem to be much of the *Lizzie*. She was but a little raft to drift out on those tides which move among the stars. " Now's your chance," said her crew, and I took it, on all fours. The last remnant of London was then pushed from us with a pole. We were launched on night, which had begun its ebb towards morning.

The punt sidled away obliquely for mid-stream. I stood at one end of it. The figure of Charon could be seen at the other, of long acquaintance with this passage, using his sweep with the indifference of habitude. Perhaps it was not

Charon. Yet there was some obstruction to the belief that we were bound for no more than the steamer *Aldebaran*, anchored in Bugsby's Reach. From the low deck of the barge it was surprising that the River, whose name was Night, was content with the height to which it had risen. Perhaps it was taking its time. It might soon receive an influx from space, rise then in a silent upheaval, and those low shadows that were London, even now half-foundered, would at once go. This darkness was an irresponsible power. It was the same flood which had sunk Knossos and Memphis. It was tranquil, indifferent, knowing us not, reckoning us all one with the Sumerians. They were below it. It had risen above them. Now the time had come when it was laving the base of London.

The crew cried out to us that over there was the entrance to the West India Dock. We knew that place in another life. But should Charon joke with us ? We saw only chaos, in which the beams from a reputed city glimmered without purpose.

The shadow of the master of our black barge pulled at his sweep with a slow confidence that was fearful amid what was sightless and unknown. His pipe glowed, as with the profanity of an immortal to whom eternity and infinity are of the usual significance. Then a red and green eye appeared astern and there was a steady throbbing as if some monster were in pursuit of us. A tug shaped near us, drew level, and exposed with its fires, as it went ahead, a radiant *Lizzie* on an area of water that leaped in red flames. The furnace door of the tug was shut, and at once we

38

were blind. " Hold hard," yelled our skipper, and the *Lizzie* slipped into the turmoil of the tug's wake.

There would be Millwall. The tug and the turmoil had gone. We were alone again in the beyond. There was no sound now but the water spattering under our craft, and the fumbling and infrequent splash of the sweep. Once we heard the miniature bark of a dog, distinct and fine, as though the distance had refined it as well as reduced it. We were nearly round the loop the River makes about Millwall, and this unknown region before us was Blackwall Reach by day, and Execution Dock used to be dead ahead. To the east, over the waters, red light exploded fan-wise and pulsed on the clouds latent above, giving them momentary form. It was as though, from the place where it starts, the dawn had been released too soon, and was at once recalled. " The gas works," said the skipper.

Still the slow drift, quite proper to those at large in eternity. But this, I was told, was the beginning of Bugsby's Reach. It was a first premonition, then a doubt, and at last a distinct tremor in the darkness ahead of us. A light appeared, grew nearer, higher, and brighter, and there was a suspicion of imminent mass. " Watch her," warned the skipper. Watch what ? There was nothing to watch but the dark and some planets far away, one of them red. The menacing one still grew higher and brighter. It came at us. A wall instantly appeared to overhang us, with a funnel and masts above it, and our skipper's yell was lost in the thunder of a churning propeller. The air shuddered, and a siren hooted in the heavens. A long dark body seemed minutes going by us, and our skipper's insults were taken in silence by her superior deck. She left us riotous in her wake, and we continued our journey dancing our indignation on the uneasy deck of the *Lizzie*.

The silent drift recommenced, and we neared a region of unearthly lights and the smell of sulphur, where aerial skeletons, vast and black, and columns and towers, alternately glowed and vanished as the doors of infernal fires were opened and shut. We drew abreast of this phantom place where flames and darkness battled amid gigantic ruin. Charon spoke. "They're the coal wharves," he said.

The lights of a steamer rise in the night below the wharves, but it was our own progress which brought them nearer. She was anchored. We made out at last her shape, but at first she did not answer our hail.

"Hallo, *Aldebaran*," once more roared our captain.

There was no answer. In a minute we should be by her, and too late.

"Barge ahoy!" came a voice. "Look out for a line."

THE SEVEN AGES

Ian Hay

CLAPHAM COMMON, as such, may not sound romantic or distinctive. To the aristocrats of Clerkenwell, for instance, Clapham, Brixton, Surbiton, Peckham, Balham, Streatham, and Hoxton are all identical and inseparable items in a howling wilderness called South London. But Clapham Common on a fine Saturday afternoon in April is a very fair reproduction of the Elysian Fields, for the simple reason that every one there is doing the thing he likes best. Play may be defined as that form of hard work which appeals to us most ; and here we are, putting our hearts into it, whether we be old or young.

All the Seven Ages of Man are represented.

First, the Infant—that is to say, human beings so young as to require an attendant. These are everywhere—staggering, crawling, being carried, being dragged, or being trundled magnificently in perambulators, usually by shrewish and voluble little girls. Whenever the perambulator comes to anchor amid a flotilla of other perambulators its occupant is lowered over the side and permitted a short cruise in the open, unaccompanied.

The diversions of a Clapham Common baby

appear to be threefold. First, rising on its hind-legs and remaining there for one breathless moment, thereafter pitching forward to tearful disaster, or else subsiding backwards with a terrific but apparently painless bump ; secondly, engaging in battle with other infants of similar tonnage and armament ; thirdly, eating mud.

The next size of child is just large enough, quite literally, to paddle its own canoe. In the small round pond (possibly as deep as eighteen inches in the middle) you may behold a great concourse of shipping. Each ship is just large enough to contain one extremely small passenger—or rather, one captain, engineer, and crew combined. He operates a horizontal crank with his hands, and thus turns a pair of miniature paddle-wheels which propel his craft, at a rate inversely proportional to the amount of splash, in divers directions. This type of vessel has no rudder, and collisions are frequent. Fortunately the rate of speed is low, and the loss of tonnage is not serious. Female relatives, chanting a chorus of admonition and reproof, form a melodious ring round the pond.

The third class consists of small boys of about ten, too young to be entirely exempt from petti-coat supervision, but old enough and sinful enough to be able to dodge it fairly consistently. They climb such trees as they can find, play catch with one another—to a sisterly accompaniment of " butter-fingers ! " and " fat 'ead ! "—if they own a ball ; or retrieve balls for other people if they do not. A few of them possess one roller-skate, upon which they propel themselves with astonishing speed and some lack of definite direction—as meditative pedestrians have occasion to discover.

Then come the emancipated ages—the Warrior class—the players of football and cricket. Both these games are being played here to-day, side by side. To a certain extent they overlap. A moment ago a googly bowler in a cricket match just beside us bowled a quite phenomenal wide right into the middle of an adjacent football match, just as the ball from the football match, soaring high into touch out of the field of play, spread-eagled all the wickets of the batsman in the cricket match. However, fair exchange is no robbery.

The football players fall into two categories— Recognized and Unrecognized. The Recognized occupy more space and enjoy more privileges than any other combatants on the Common. Each match—and there are scores of them—is played upon a comparatively rectangular piece of ground, with real goal posts, their tops joined by a tape ; and the players wear regulation football kit, including club colours which put the spring flowers to shame. There are even touch judges, a referee, and spectators. Probably the two teams have names — the Battersea Park Hornets, we will say, as against the Vampires of Tooting Bec. Possibly the result of the match will be published in to-morrow's Sunday papers. Good luck to them both !

But wherever we may bestow our admiration, our sympathy goes out to the Fifth Age, the Unrecognized. They do not seem to play any worse than their more favoured brethren ; but apparently they lack the numbers, or the means, or the influence, to stage a full-dress battle. They play with their trousers tucked into their socks, upon an irregular polygon of ground much obstructed by trees and notice boards; their goal posts are represented by heaps of coats, and doubtful points as they arise are decided not by a referee, but by mutual recrimination. One would like to find a complete ground for them, with goals and colours like the rest. But perhaps they are merely undergoing a period of probation, and will ultimately rise to higher things. Good luck to them too, for they, beyond all present, are playing the game for its own sake.

The irregularities of the ground whereon they play calls to mind a certain public park in distant Edinburgh, where many of the " fitba' " pitches are set upon the side of a considerable hill. Here, if you lose the toss, you will have, quite literally, an uphill battle to fight. But your turn will come after half-time. It is no uncommon thing in these heroic combats for a side to change ends twelve or fifteen goals down, and win the match.

The Sixth Age takes itself very seriously. It consists of middle-aged gentlemen of preoccupied appearance, who sail model yachts in the largest pond. They arrive from all quarters early in the afternoon, carrying their yachts; sometimes the yacht is wheeled in a perambulator, followed by an indignant and bandy-legged baby, walking. Obviously they have hurried home from the week's work and eaten their dinner with forced calm ; after which their wives have lifted down the recently dusted *Britannia* or *Valkyrie* from the shelf and deposited it in the arms of its owner, saying, with an indulgent smile :

44

" There now, run off to the pond, and don't get your feet wet ; and don't let me see you back here again before six o'clock ! "

They are beautifully made, some of these little yachts, and their fitting and rigging have obviously been a matter of loving care through many a winter evening. There is an ingenious arrangement which enables you to fix the rudder in any position, and so counteract the natural tendency of a fore-and-aft rigged boat to luff up into the eye of the wind.

Here is a race starting now, between *Shamrock* and *Bluebell*. The respective owners are an uncommunicative man in pince-nez, and an old gentleman in a species of yachting cap, obviously an enthusiast of several generations' standing. The yachts' names are painted upon their little companionways, and each sports a small burgee marked C.M.Y.C., which stands, presumably, for " Clapham Model Yacht Club "—or, possibly, " Clapham Makes You a Commodore."

The procedure is simple. The boats are pushed off from the lower end of the pond, and the one which reaches the other end first is the winner. Hypnotic control of rudders not yet having been introduced into yachting practice, this achievement sometimes takes time. Sometimes—usually—a yacht runs ashore half-way up the pond ; you are then permitted to prod it in the required direction with a stick and push it out again—repeating the operation as often as may be necessary until the goal is reached.

Plainly no small skill and knowledge are required in the exact adjustment of the sails. To-day, for instance, the breeze is blowing diagonally down the pond, and progress can best be achieved by alternate long reaches and short beats. Consequently, by an ingenious arrangement of the mainsheet, the good ship *Shamrock*, while upon the starboard tack, is given a comparatively loose rein ; but when put about after her first beaching and sent off into the teeth of the wind upon the other tack, she finds herself so close hauled that after beating out ten yards or so she goes about of her own volition, and accomplishes another rapid and profitable reach upon the starboard tack.

Ultimately *Shamrock* wins the race, for *Bluebell* rams a strange craft *en route*—which is not altogether surprising, considering the congestion of traffic. The pair, with their riggings locked inextricably together, drift ignominiously towards the bank, and are finally recovered by the ancient device of casting stones into the water just beyond them—an operation in which several volunteers from Class Three co-operate enthusiastically, if not always entirely acceptably.

And the Seventh Age ? There it is, sitting in the lee of that hedge—a dozen sedate and mainly elderly gentlemen, bowed over chess - boards, draught - boards, domino - boards — oblivious to their surroundings and the intensely wise comments of the spectators. The spring has brought them, even them, out under the open sky.

They are not all elderly, though. Note this player here—a youngish, soldierly man, playing dominoes. We note that he makes all his moves with his right hand. His left hand, or rather his empty sleeve, is tucked neatly into his coat pocket. Perhaps, if the truth were known, his heart is out among the Warriors, upon one of the football pitches. If so, he does not show it. He smiles resolutely upon his elders, does the thing that's nearest, and plays the double six.

A WORD TO THE AMATEURS

James Agate

To my way of thinking there is no such thing as
" amateur " acting. A wit of the 'nineties said
that there is no such thing as good or bad people.
" People," he said, " are either charming or
tedious. That is all there is to be said about
people." My view is that acting is either agreeable or boring, and that the question of professional or amateur status does not come in.
But one cannot shut one's eyes to the fact that a
state of mind exists wherein numbers of people,
otherwise normally constituted, band themselves
together for the performance of plays in public,
without remuneration.

The love of acting is probably one of the earliest
manifestations of the human spirit. Mr. Kipling
has told us of the time when first the

> ". . . spoken word Man's Spirit stirred
> Beyond his belly need."

Let me suggest that an early use of the word
and the spirit-stirrings was to put two and two
together and make, probably a song to begin
with, and next a play about a mighty hunter
returning quarry laden to his cave and his adoring
mate. Throughout the ages the first desire of the

48

child, beyond his tummy's need, has been to be told a story ; the second, to act one. It is a commonplace that children act over again, in their own persons, the lives of the heroes and the heroines of the stories read aloud to them in the nursery, and so become, for the time being, the " Heir of Redclyffe," or the young woman in " The Lamplighter " whose name I always forget.

Granted, then, that play-acting is an ineradicable impulse in human nature, let us take a look at the amateur dramatic societies which are the intellectual life not only of the countryside, but also of places such as Wigan, Peebles, Paisley, and Golders Green. *To whom do the performances give pleasure ?* Æsthetic pleasure, I mean, and not the mischievous delight of watching the Squire's son make love to the Vicar's daughter, and whispering that they are " sweet " on one another in real life. In my view, the pleasure conferred by amateur acting is upon the actors themselves. The recollection comes to me here of a scene not from real life but from Balzac. At a *soirée* the little ninny, Céleste Colleville, has pleaded a cold in order not to be obliged to sing after some operatic star. To this her mother replies : " One sings as one sings. Every voice has its merits ! " Whereupon the ninny's father, who has just lost twenty francs at gambling, replies to her mother savagely : " My dear, you talk like a *bourgeoise*. One sings with a voice on condition that one has a voice to sing with. But one does not sing after a great diva ! " That is the whole point.

Now, to consider the matter from the point of view of the amateur actor. I read somewhere the other day a sentence which struck me as almost monstrously foolish. This was the sentence : " Amateur dramatic societies are springing up all over the country, pointing to and developing increased civic and moral sense." I should like the writer of that sentence to visit the dressing-room of any amateur about to perform *David Garrick*, and getting himself into the breeches of that hero. I should then like to ask him what signs he observed in that actor of increased and developed civic and moral sense. An old professional actor, whose opinion I once asked about amateur dramatic societies, pondered a while, and then gloomily replied : " Well, they can't be as bad as amateur operatic societies—and, of course, they can always play *David Garrick*! It won't do them any harm, and the old play can stand it."

To perform any play of the order of *David Garrick, Sweet Lavender, Mice and Men*, and so forth, cannot possibly do the actor any good, while to suggest that the audience can get any of the right kind of fun out of it is pure nonsense.

" Paint the soul, never mind the legs and arms ! " wrote Browning. Which is rather like telling some coachman to drive his horse and never mind the reins and whip ; or some cricketer to play the game and never mind the bat and ball. But poets are like that, and one understands what Browning meant. Inasmuch as amateur actors never know what to do with their legs and arms, my advice to them is, and always has been, to concentrate upon plays of soul. " To know Hermann Melville," wrote Viola Meynell, " is to be partly made of him for ever," and for the amateur to act in good plays is to be partly made of their authors for ever. That is why I advise amateurs to play any of the pieces of Tchehov, Granville-Barker, Hauptmann, Sudermann, Masefield, Munro, O'Neill, Claudel, Maugham, Pirandello, Vildrac, Yeats, Schnitzler, Barrie, Synge, and Ibsen. There is an old saying that you may as well be hanged for a sheep as a lamb, and I think that this holds tremendously true of amateur dramatic societies.

"But how," the amateur may ask, "shall I get an audience to come and watch my attempts at the sublime which, invigorating though they may be to me, must to them be enervating and ridiculous?" I think there is an answer to that. Probably the amateur juggler who tried to keep an umbrella, a cigar, a top-hat, three tennis balls, and a bit of paper all in the air at the same time would come a complete and ignominious cropper, because he has not got that particular kind of dexterity. But if he be told to roll a big stone uphill, and if he move it by so much as an inch, he has still done something, and we can see that he has done something. It is the same with the play. I would rather see an amateur tackle what looks like the perfectly impossible part of King Lear than one of Mr. Seymour Hicks's airy trifles; he would at least do something with the one and nothing with the other, for in the first case he would be at the least reciting and therefore bringing back to recollection ennobled and beautiful lines, whereas, in the other, he would be failing to catch something which is only worth doing when it is done by a Hicks or a Sacha Guitry. Stevenson said—and the quotation is particularly helpful to the amateur actor—that

" a spirit comes out of the man who means execution, which outlives the most untimely ending." For " untimely ending " let us read " indifferent accomplishment." In other words, it is better to shoot at a great work and miss it, than to bring down a mere trifle.

The best kind of amateur theatricals are country house theatricals, and I do not know any better expression of their excitement than the following stanzas by that perfect little master, Winthrop Mackworth Praed :

> " Come, Clarence, it's really enchanting
> To listen and look at the rout,
> We're all of us puffing and panting,
> And raving and running about ;
> Here Kitty and Adelaide bustle ;
> There Andrew and Anthony bawl ;
> Flutes murmur—chains rattle—robes rustle
> In chorus at Fustian Hall."

The poet urges his friend Clarence to do this and do that to make the affair at the Hall a success :

> " And then for our funeral procession,
> Pray get us a love of a pall—
> Or how shall we make an impression
> On feelings, at Fustian Hall ? "

" Love of a pall " is a love of a phrase, and because of it I, personally, am prepared to forgive the telescoping of " funeral " in the first line. Clarence is next told that his " idol Albina " will make a success, since " We all think there never was seen a Performer so like the O'Neill." Praed was born in 1802, and died at the age of thirty-six. The poem was probably written in the late 'twenties, during which period the Town was raving over Miss O'Neill, whom so astute a judge of acting as Hazlitt rated very highly.

As for Albina, Clarence is told that

> " At rehearsals her exquisite fury
> Has amply affected us all ;
> For one tear that trickles at Drury
> There'll be twenty at Fustian Hall."

To quote is, at best, a temptation to which all of us sometime must fall ; at the worst it's no mere relaxation, but a vice which still holds us in thrall. Even to the extent of making one's own sober prose jig to the measure of the man we are quoting. I hope the reader will forgive one more stanza, which I cannot resist giving, and for two reasons. First, the fun of it ; second, the sentimental reflection that it must be many years since Praed was trotted out. This is it :

> " And, Clarence, you'll really delight us,
> If you'll do your endeavour to bring,
> From the Club, a young person to write us
> Our prologue, and that sort of thing.
> Poor Crotchet, who did them supremely,
> Is gone for a Judge to Bengal ;
> I fear we shall miss him extremely
> This season, at Fustian Hall."

Here, again, I think the country-house atmosphere is perfectly maintained.

JOYS OF THE STREET

C. E. Montague

"Within this hour it will be dinner-time :
Till that, I'll view the manners of the town,
Peruse the traders, gaze upon the buildings,
And then return, and sleep within mine inn."
Comedy of Errors, I., ii., 12.

I

THERE are islands in the Pacific where one of
your prime aims in life is not to be killed in your
bed the next time your house is blown down by
a hurricane. The hurricanes come at intervals of
a few years ; even earthquakes are quite on the
cards ; however your house may be built, it will
have to come down. And so, when people build
in those parts, they do not try to put up any
cloud-capped towers or gorgeous palaces of stone ;
better far to have one side of a light match-box
fall in on your head while you sleep than to have
the most handsomely vaulted roof of massy
marble or veined alabaster do the same thing.
So the houses are built lightly of wood, the whole
of each on one floor. If they have to be big, as
a hospital has, they are made with a rich abundance
of doors, so that, as soon as the air of the earth is
smitten with frenzy, all the more helpless inmates

54

can be swiftly carried out and laid down in the open. As you would imagine, the architecture of places like this has a vivid eloquence of its own. To the reconnoitring eyes on every approaching ship it cries out the severe conditions on which life is retained in that island.

Other architecture may be less vociferous. But all architecture talks, and should talk, from the first to the last. The earliest Egyptian buildings speak freely about both sacred and secular things. We might have gathered from these informants alone, if we had not known it in other ways, that it was a very serious affair for an Egyptian, in his opinion, if his body were not left in a safe place after his death. When a man died, his soul, unless he had been good, was to go the round of various beasts, as a tenant of their several bodies. If he was good, his soul was to leave him for the time, spend three thousand years in the society of the divine Osiris, and then come back to the same earthen tenement that it had quitted. Naturally an Egyptian architect, when he had to design a tomb, made sure that, whatever less practical grace it might lack, it would last out three thousand years good and so keep his client's embalmed body intact and fit for the soul to re-enter. Hence the fantastic solidity of a pyramid.

The chief secular thing that the greatest Egyptian architecture expressed was, I suppose, a primitive pride of conquest, cruel and vulgar. It seems that about the seventeenth century B.C. the rulers of Egypt became a somewhat Prussian-istic set of believers in war as good business and not as a dire occasional necessity only. They went a-hunting their neighbours, brought back

55

hordes of them, taken alive, and used them as slaves. They were such a supply of cheap labour as no kings, so far as we know, had ever had at their disposal before. The slave-raiding record was beaten, and architecture had to commemorate the glorious performance. Clearly the most expressive way to do this was to build in such a fashion as nobody could have attempted who had not got the use of an unprecedented multitude of unpaid workmen. Hence a wanton massiveness of build, a swaggering amplitude of waste. It is the pride of all art, when in health, to take the simplest means to its ends. Here was an art, sick with pandering to sick souls, that has shown the world ever since how slight an achievement may be in proportion to all the toil that has gone to bring it off.

But some one may say : " Yes, architecture talks, and tells us interesting things—except in England, and now. We had an English architecture once. The men who built the cathedrals of Lincoln and Peterborough, Wells and Lichfield, had some sort of kinship, no doubt, in their art with the men who were building at Chartres, Amiens, Rheims, and Rouen. But still they were English. Their buildings speak English, the English of their day. So does the work of our best painters and draughtsmen speak the English of to-day. But our architects ! They seem to be like denationalized poets or painters who should set out to write a poem or paint a picture by saying to themselves : ' Now, shall I write this poem in the style of the Greek Anthology ? Or of the Italian Renaissance ? Or of the French Romantic epoch ? ' Or ' Shall I paint this picture

in the style of the Byzantines ? Or of the
Venetians ? Or of the great Dutchmen ? ' What
expressiveness is there for us common Englishry
in some accomplished person's scholarly exercises
in Classical, Gothic, Palladian and other alien
architectural styles ? "

Well, there may be something in that. And
yet the expressiveness of anything built to serve
a human purpose, or that of a beaver or wren, is
too eager to be easily gagged. You may travel
after dark in winter through the textile counties
in the north and know when you are entering a
cotton-spinning region by the broad and lofty
detached groups of hundreds of windows blazing
with light, and when you pass into a weaving
district by the wide, low expanses of sky-lighted
sheds prone on the ground, their electric light
showing dimly through the ground glass of their
roofs. You may even tell by the relative sizes of
those Aladdin's palaces, outlined on a ground of
darkness by their own flare of brilliant windows,
whether you are in a land of spinners of " fine
counts," like Bolton, or " coarse counts," like
Oldham. But by day every town in all the
smutty Pleiades of English towns becomes an
individual face, unlike every other, and piquantly
scored, as a human face is, with records of its life
and marks of the labours or hobbies that have
engrossed it

II

Go to Liverpool or Manchester. Issue from
your station of arrival and look about you. If
you have only the commonplace well-to-do

Englishman's eye that the standard of education of his kind has dimmed, you may find the cities much alike. " Simply warehouses, everywhere," you may say, not knowing what rubbish you say. If, by the grace of God or the help of a friend, you have escaped mal-education, you will observe that in each city a warehouse means a different thing. The warehouses of Liverpool are huge strong-boxes of brick, aired and half-lit by a small number of windows, and entered by the least gracious of practicable doors. Massive, sombre, and grim, these buildings seem to disclaim airs and graces ; they say " If you don't like our looks, keep away. We don't want you." And, since anything that a building says frankly and firmly has interest, no typical Liverpool warehouse is dull.

The typical Manchester warehouse says nothing like that. It has a welcoming entrance ; its architect has designed this portal to exercise an inward suction, like the hospitable doors of inns and urbane private dwellings. Pains have clearly been taken to make all its rooms lightsome. Outside, it attempts, and often achieves, an air of dignity and a large unity. At its best it looks handsome and rich, but in a sober way, with composure and an impressive reserve.

These characters of brick and stone tell you that Liverpool is a place of transhipment and storage, and Manchester a wholesale mart. The " big barrack warehouse " which the half blind see everywhere in either city, is in the one case a lock-up, in the other a showroom. And yet not a shop. In a Manchester textile warehouse things are being bought and sold all day, but not as in a shop. Both parties to every transaction are expert professionals. So catch-penny tricks are of no use. The vendor is like a barrister arguing before a judge sitting alone, and not to a jury. Nothing is here to be gained by the little dodges of window display that draw the poor impressionable amateur like you or me on to the premises of a hosier. All that wise building can do, within, to promote the business in hand, is to admit the customer with a kind of stately geniality and then to make his movements about the interior easy, his light for examining goods abundant, and his impression of the firm's assured solidity profound. In the exterior it can give promise of those practical blessings within, and it can especially express the reposeful solvency of the business, its ample reserves, its princely rank among merchants, its resolution to stay in the trade not for an age but for all time. Nothing of all this is needed to keep heavy merchandise dry and safe from thieves between its sojourns in a ship and in a train. So both kinds of warehouse are good. Both speak the truth about their intentions. But they are different, and, to the ear that cares to listen to them both, such differences are delicious.

Leaving the warehouses, look at the banks. Every good bank is, at heart, like the first bank of all, the snugly defensible cave, with a stout stockade in its front, where a personable cave-man, club in hand, stood guard over the deposited flint treasures of the absent. It is a strong room ; it ought to look it ; and it often does. There is in Mosley Street in Manchester a model of a great bank building, the work of Edward

Walters, a local nineteenth-century architect as truly a master as the author of the modern theatre at Amiens. It makes you feel inclined to leave your money there, and all your plate too. It fills you with a sense of massive, world-defying security such as you get from the Strozzi Palace at Florence, and yet it is not lumbering; it has grace and the scholarship that we cannot do without now if we would; and beside it there sits, square and grave, a real modern town mansion.

Not, mind you, that diverting product of conflicting emotions, a country house in a town. Many Englishmen of wealth have built themselves country houses in town. Driven by custom or some ambition to live in London for part of the year, these Nimrods in exile have treated themselves to such aid as architectural genius could give them in dreaming they were not wholly cut off from the fox and the partridge. So, we suppose, there came into being such mansions as Crewe House, in Curzon Street—long and low, and separated from the street by a kind of diminutive park, with a drive. They look like intended embodiments of unreason. They waste priceless land, and they spoil the line of a street; and all, it would seem, to provide some spacious caterwauling places for the region cats. Yet, viewed with the tenderness that can understand and forgive, they may express the poignant emotion of some broad-acred Squire Western, dragged reluctantly to town for a few months; his womankind have done it, and the poor man languishes here for the views from his justice-room in distant Cheshire or Somerset. The late eighteenth-century novel and play tell of a species of civil warfare apparently endemic among the rural gentry ; the wife and daughters ever and anon put up a fight for a seasonal descent upon the capital and all its social joys ; the obdurate male vows that, for moral, æsthetic, and financial reasons, nothing shall move him this year. " Budge," says the landowner's lady, with daughters to marry. " Budge not," says the landowner's heart ; " stay with the game and the turnips, where you are safe." Some well-to-do couples, we may imagine, compromised on a sham country house in the capital.

Even now these mongrel habitations seem to inspire little shame in many of those who ought to know most of the points of a thoroughbred house. You will sometimes see " a country house in London " almost proudly advertised for sale by some eminent auctioneer who would think twice or three times before recommending to buyers " a town house in the New Forest." The true town house, like that I spoke of, is always contained, urbane and unfreakish. It frankly accepts the close propinquity of its fellows, and bows to the necessity of more or less uniformity with them. It does not shirk, but delights in, the immediate contact of the street and the piquant interposition of only some inches of brick or a lamina of glass between the intimacies of the private life and public pavements where east winds are whirling straws and old rags of paper about in eddies of dust. Like any Palace over the Grand Canal, it overcomes triumphantly the severe conditions that it shall have only one façade to show, that three of its four sides shall be out of your sight, and two of them blind. And if it be the official house of a banker it will look banker-like and nothing else. You may just remember the time when men of courtesy, on going into the bank where they kept their accounts, would take off their hats, the bank being still, to their sense, the parlour of a trusted professional friend and adviser whom they were calling upon. Indeed it almost was. Most banks were still private ones. Most bankers were still living over their banks. And the houses in which they both lived and did business expressed, when well built, not only the strength of a safe but the attributes of good sound men to bank with. Not grandiose or showy, but dignified in design and betraying no dismay at the cost of the best material, neither aping the abodes of " the quality " nor dissembling the possession of ample reserve funds, they fortified your faith that the head of Mr. Heywood was not to be easily turned, or that, whatever happened, Mr. Parr, at any rate, would never let you down.

III

As you go north from the centre of Oxford, along the wide boulevard of St. Giles and the Banbury or the Woodstock Road, you traverse, for several hundred yards of your walk, a region in which no one style of building prevails. There are houses that speak of the early nineteenth century, of the late and early eighteenth, and even of more distant dates. There are houses that seem, to this day, to be trying to save

window-tax. There are a few huddled and cower-
ing houses that look as if they had the weather
or some other form of external menace much on
their minds. And there are august and affable
houses, like the old Judges' Lodging, consciously
and securely the homes of people of consequence.
" As I'm a person," old Lady Wishfort would
swear, and, if such houses swore, their oaths would
be like hers.

Out of this zone of diversity in age and in make
you pass into a zone that wears a more uniform
air. Here half the houses set you thinking of
some Venetian Gothic façade. The pointed
arches over their porches murmur fondly of the
thirteenth century. The windows of the servants'
bedrooms are bisected vertically by little columns
of marble. The conscientious constructor of
wooden toy horses always strove " to come as
near to Natur as I can for sixpence." So, to
the sensitive eye and feeling heart, do these
modern villas plead that under serious difficulties
they are doing their best to resemble the Loredan
Palace or the Ca' d'Oro or some other model of
architectural virtue fronting the Grand Canal.
This zone, as memory recalls it, is rather cold
and grave in colour. It presents to your view
many slates.

You emerge from it almost abruptly, to enter
a third zone. Here fealty is sworn to no Doges,
but to Queen Anne. The whole quarter wears
a warm flush. The walls are of a buxom red.
Many roofs are red-tiled. Some of these roofs
are of generous extent, their tops flouting the sky
like Norwegian banners, while their skirts offer to
descend to the ground ; they sometimes suggest

that the architect's dearest wish was to let no man suffer from any shortage of box-rooms. Some of the chimneys are treated with much gusto and fancy ; they must have given to their authors many amusing hours. Nearly all the woodwork is white ; the whole colour scheme is the simple and chaste one seen in the Countess Olivia's face,

> ". . . whose red and white
> Nature's own sweet and cunning hand laid on."

Remembering man's thrifty habit of building his habitation out of whatever material the soil presents on the spot, you may wonder, as you go on walking northward, whether, perhaps, some strange and serious geological " fault " has struck at right angles across the Banbury and Woodstock Roads. Can it be that a quarter or half a mile north of St. Giles's Church the Oxford Clay of the geologists has abruptly come to an end and a bed of red sandstone has succeeded it in the position of top layer ? Northerners, living on solid stone, have their houses stone-coloured ; Notts and South Derbyshire men, children of the ruddy Keuper Marl, live in houses equally ruddy ; Londoners, the nurslings of sundry new-fangled Eocene clays, acquiesce in a corresponding range of unsightly brick, extending from the turbidly purple to the wanly bilious. Here, in the neighbourhood of Somerville College, do we, then, stand on one of the frontier cracks in the crust of the earth.

But, even while you muse, you pass out once more from zone into zone. In the new belt Queen Anne is indeed dead. Red brick is succeeded by greyish roughcast, or even by whitewash. The frames of windows sink in till they are flush with the walls. A conscious, conscientious plainness, a proud and rugged humility reigns. Here the Englishman's house is no longer entitled, like other castles, " Belvoir " or " Norham " upon the front gate, but " The Croft," " The Shack," or " The Sheiling." The dignity of honest toil, the joy of plain living, the charm of " The Cottar's Saturday Night " and some other beautiful thoughts come into your mind as you traverse this zone of agreeable villas that make as if to escape in disguise as labourers' cottages.

Out beyond these are the open fields, waiting for yet other ripples of architectural invention or revival to break over them, sped outwards from the centre and power-house of æsthetic activity, somewhere in the neighbourhood of the Sheldonian and the Bodleian. Still, four sharply bordered zones are pretty good, to begin with. And these are as clear as the similar rings that you see in the sawn trunk of a tree, examined in section. Like those annular grainings they tell you a good many things, important or diverting. The grainings will tell you the age of the tree ; they record what years of its life were lean and hard to live in, from want of rain or of sun ; they keep a note of the time when some bad accident deranged the tree's growth, when it was half starved by an extensive exposure of its roots, or when some wholesale lopping of its upper branches left its trunk overstocked with sap for the year, and set the stuff bursting out in a crowd of unnatural boughs low down on the stem. So the first slowly grown ring of houses round Oxford expresses the great

stretch of time for which the university, mediæval
and monastic still, created little or no need of
genteel house-room outside its colleges and halls.
The second ring, the ring of thronging villas
tinged with Venetian Gothic art, expresses at
once the new liberty given to Fellows to marry,
the conscious, sensitive and slightly fashion-ridden
culture of the first community of married Fellows
and their wives, and the immense ascendancy of
Ruskin over the educated minds of his time,
especially the academic ones. The third, the
Queen Anne ring, reports the mighty change of
critical mode which followed. The yoke of
Ruskin was thrown off ; the taboo upon Renaissance and post-Renaissance architecture was
denounced ; the excess of dilettantism, affectation,
and pastiche in the less excellent work of the
Gothic revival added force to a reaction which,
anyhow, had to come, man being by nature un-
stable as water, not wholly to his disadvantage.

About the same time Oxford was becoming,
socially, less isolated and autonomous, more an
ordinary portion of middle-class England ; many
quite unacademic specimens of that England,
indeed, were now using her as a Cheltenham or
a Bedford, and filling the yard of her railway
station with shiny private carriages where there
had once been nothing but the few and frowsy
hansoms proper to poverty and learning. So
suburban Oxford, in the second generation of the
married don, fell easily in with the new architectural fashion then speckling the Surrey hills
with the red bricks and tiles and bright white
doors and window sashes of the Queen Anne
style, as it was called, whatever a Queen Anne

ghost might think of some of its gambols and fanfaronades. Then, in the due course of time, it became rather the exquisite note to be consciously poor. To be in the height of the fashion you had to be sorely stricken in purse by Mr. Lloyd George's notoriously depredatory taxes on land. At the same time, advanced liberal speculation was carrying part of the well-to-do classes into a mood of theoretic sympathy with the classes engaged in manual labour. So, from two directions at once, gentle winds of inspiration began to converge on the art of the architect. A magnified labourer's cottage, roughcast and severe, could express either the indignant or the enthusiastic descent of the occupant from the exalted level of those who do not toil nor spin. You could live in a pleasant hovel so as to let it cry aloud to the world either " See what the Radical thieves have reduced me to," or " See the cross that I bear, out of my love for the poor." So easily and entertainingly may social history be studied in those gossipy pages, the fronts of suburban villas.

IV

No sort of weather, of course, can be dull anywhere—not even a great thaw—unless you have a dull mind to help it to bore you. But some sorts of weather are even more exciting than others. Most exciting of all, perhaps, in a city, are the first hours of romantic strangeness after a heavy fall of snow. While snow lies deep, the proportions of things are altered. Streets become much wider, especially if it be Sunday and not many people about. For the frontier between footpath and road is wiped out. Women look tallest in dresses with no horizontal lines of flounces or reefs round their skirts ; in the same way a street widens out as soon as its width is not cut up into strips by the kerbs. Most city streets look much the better for this work of deletion. Their modern buildings commonly exceed in height the total width of roadway and footpaths. Thus they lose an element of handsomeness of which even the most squalid buildings cannot altogether deprive a broad street through a slum. Some part of this lost handsomeness returns when a deep coating of snow, still untrodden, has made this surprising and charming addition to the width from house to house. It is as if every street had been improved, for good, by a miraculous setting back of the front on each side.

Another engaging and curious effect of snow in towns is the emphasis suddenly laid upon all visible roofs. Within a few minutes the upper part of a Gothic town hall may become a system of steep hanging snow-slopes, like a Chamonix aiguille ; they call out to be climbed or—it is much the same thing—to have their gradients considered. You may have never thought about city chimneys before : but now they present themselves to you in sharp black relief against those white sheets of snow-covered slate. They will not be denied. They appeal for fair play. They ask, have architects done chimneys justice ? Or have they all this time been scornfully trusting the wretched lay citizen not to look up at any sky-line when he walks abroad ?

Eye and mind are entertained and stirred by

this abrupt and extensive redistribution of all the relative stresses that they have commonly laid on the component parts of a familiar scene. It imparts a piquancy akin to that which some well-known place may acquire when, for the first time, you look at it just after a clear midsummer sunrise, when all the long shadows are thrown in directions in which you have never seen them reaching out before. Of course buildings, in our climate, are not specially designed with a view to the figure that they will cut when well snowed upon. But then neither is a portrait in oils designed to be looked at upside down. And yet a painter sometimes finds it helpful to invert his canvas and see how it looks. In some such way it is not merely a lark, but a revelation or an exposure, to see how our familiar masterpieces of architecture look when the arbitrarily employed castor of the heavens has sprinkled capricious new accents on their several elements. They were not meant for such trials. Still, they ought to be able to stand them.

Another pleasant freak played by snow upon modern cities, is to mediævalize them—at any rate to illude you into the notion that it is doing so. Bond Street in London, or St. Ann's Square in Manchester, does not become, under snow, quite like the oldest parts of Chester or Tewkesbury. But the ordinary difference between them is immensely lessened. Is it that the more permanent elements in all domestic architecture are those which snow does least to mask, and that the contrast is strongest between just such orders of details as snow tends most to obliterate ? Or is it only that in our habitual mental visions of mediæval towns we are excessively inclined to imagine them snow-laden because of the traditional fondness of popular historical romance and melodrama for " Christmas weather "—Jane Shore praying in the snow, among half-timbered, many-gabled dwellings, and so on ? And that urban snow thus evokes in the common herd of us some semblance of a " residual mediæval herd-consciousness," as the learned, or at any rate the polysyllabic, would say ? Who knows ? Perhaps every architect does, all the time. I only speak as an ignoramus, gazing at the splendid show that surrounds us on these great occasions.

V

Another time when cities are above themselves and shine with a kind of blithe novelty is when a lingering spring has softened at last and summer bursts like one bud, with a jubilant suddenness, seeming to spill its whole cornucopia of colour and fragrance on some one generous morning in June. Into the centre of cities it comes, not as it does to fortunate gardens, but with a kind of indirectness. It percolates. The glamour is re-fracted. Clerks come into town with home-grown flowers in their coats, as if by agreement ; vases of roses fetched, all dewy, from suburban pleasaunces appear on the severe office tables of solicitors ; genial modifications of attire give to the incoming morning tides at the great railway termini an innocently skittish air ; the young man's awakening fancy issues in a frolic waist-coat, light in colour and weight ; portly elders have got out their sportive white toppers again and feel they are cutting rather a dash : the spirit of the wanton lapwing is abroad. In the streets the early sunshine looks curiously kind ; the air is still a little moist from the dawn, and all this radiant freshness seems to have a kind of compassion for yesterday's dust, thirsty luckless stuff that has lain all night in the streets and cannot even drink dew when it gets it. Birds in the trees of the Temple sing grace with a will for these surprising benefits ; the care-worn plane trees and elders in Wood Street, E.C., on the Embankment, and in municipal tubs are visibly taking heart to tread the round of their embarrassed bodily functions once more ; sparrows twitter from the eaves a new and braver simulation of the joy of psalmody in woods ; the very corpse of summer fragrance, embalmed and stowed away in the perfumers' shops, confesses the influence of the season—life stirs again in those mummied essences, and the massed scents seem stronger when you pass the shop, as though on such a morning you were passing their native gardens at Grasse.

Thus the wonder and glory of the season come to you at one remove ; you do not see the splendour of the June gardens and woods ; you only infer them, you hear about them, you get at them through their effect on somebody else ; they do not strike you directly but by ricochet action ; they reach you filtered and qualified, passed through one or more of those interposed media, the plump city man and his less curvilinear clerk, the grimy town bird and the struggling town tree, and even the dust on the flags. Can it be just because of that, and not in spite of it that these choice mornings in great towns have such a heart-searching loveliness ? Consider the ways of skilled novelists. These, when they strive most to move you, do not try to bring you simply face to face with the places and people and actions that they describe. They do not just tell you that this or that happened at some charming place. They invent a character to interpose between you and the scene. They give you not the place itself, but the way it affected that character. They set that character to rave or stutter about it or just gape in front of it. Homer did not try to describe Helen's face. What he did was to say how the sight of it moved even elderly men. Thackeray draws no circumstantial portrait of Beatrix Esmond ; he tells how everybody's head went round to look when she entered a box at the theatre. When Mr. Conrad has some glorious story to tell he does not tell it as coming from himself, a person knowing all ; he tells us just how much of it attracted the interest of some far more commonplace person. Why ? Because, by some subtle natural law, things come to us curiously enriched, in a certain way, when they come to us through an intervening observer or narrator. To whatever is attractive in the things themselves there is added the mysterious pleasure of deciphering the note taken of them by that actual or imaginary registrar. Mr. Kipling could have told the story of his " Love o' Women " much more fully if he had told it as an omniscient author—all authors, of course, are omniscient about their inventions. And yet he knew that he could charm us more by giving it as told by a rather ignorant and half understanding private soldier. Is there some kinship, perhaps, between the fine little psychological law which applies in that case and the curious refinement of power that summer may have to move us in cities ? For here it comes, not straight and whole but, as it were, narrated piecemeal and lamely by divers fragmentary reporters. Through her influence on pursy cit and modish spark, through her power of animating grimy sparrows and plane trees, the Lady Flora comes to us a creature of inference and mystery, even more exciting perhaps to curiosity and the creative imagination than the goddess whom we see full face, walking in all her furbelows and flounces among the flower-beds at Hampton Court and down the glades of Kew.

VI

We all see more of architecture than of any other art. Every street is a gallery of architects' work, and in most streets, whatever their age, there is good work and bad. Through these amusing shows many of us walk unperceivingly, all our days, like illiterates in a library, so richly does the fashionable education provide us with blind sides. And yet the alphabet of building is not desperately hard to learn. To make out, more or less, what a builder has tried for, how his site and surroundings have helped him or stood in his way, what means he has chosen to take to his end, out of all those that the experience of other builders has left him to choose from, what

73

kind of stuff he has built his house of, and how far he has gone to get it—all these, when once you begin, may become almost exciting subjects of speculation, without being toilfully abstruse.

The uttermost charm of a building, however, can only be got at by practising a certain shifting of your mental position, a kind of lift or displacement that shows things to you from an unaccustomed side. Every one has felt the quaint naïvety of primitive buildings. They affect us like the grand contrivances of children, their cave dwellings and tree houses which touch and amuse us with their contrast between the small creatures' great notions and their little powers. This savour is almost equally strong in ancient houses that still stand, with their eager, hampered attempts to attain some ingenuous ideal of snugness, well out of the rain, and in the wigwams and kraals of those of us who are still savages. You find it afresh wherever people are thrown out, as it were, naked on the earth again, to tend for themselves from the beginning. See the infant architecture of dug-outs in war, and of shacks that men, left to live in houseless wastes, immediately begin to make of biscuit-tins and old soap-boxes. They reek with this touching interest of the weak, contriving little animal struggling like ants or a beaver set down in a strange and bad place to get things going decently around him. How cunningly he sheaths the wet south-western wall with rags of old tin ! And how on earth will he manage the chimney ? Pitifully short of tools, materials, time, and knowledge, the dauntless creatures toil and blunder on in pursuit of some vision of their own ; we view their handiwork

long afterwards with something like the curiosity
and tenderness of mothers examining their sleeping children's vast enterprises of building in sand.

As surely as an ancient cottage possesses that
moving quaintness for us, so surely will our
buildings of to-day have some of it as soon as a
few centuries have made part of our mechanical
difficulties obsolete, and shown some of our
methods to be circuitous means to simple ends.
Buildings that people will treasure for their
quaintness in five hundred years are going up
to-day ; and Kingsway, perhaps, is founding a
rude picturesque ancientry which people will go
to see as they go now to walk on the walls of
Conway and to see the Chester Rows. Why should
we not achieve some transportation of ourselves,
in thought, to the point from which these unborn
spectators will see our offices and homes ? The
thing is feasible. It has been done. Charles
Lamb could go about the London of his day with
just that pensive, penetrating sense of the curious
human expressiveness of the place which we feel
in the Old Town at Edinburgh, or in Ravenna.
With an affection only less poignant than that of
mothers, who can sometimes see already in their
new-born infants the greyness and the wrinkles
that will come, Lamb could anticipate in imagination the gradual deposits of time and see his
contemporary London with all the emotional
creepers already clinging about it which seem to
ourselves to have grown since he died. If we
can only do that, no modern street will be dull,
and the rawest new house may have already
something of the fascination that it will assuredly
have if it stands till the year 3000.

At any rate a little sympathy will disengage from a new building its indestructible interest as a contrivance, and a term in a long series of contrivances, every term in the series becoming rather winningly childlike as soon as a few more terms have followed it. Little effort is needed to see that childlike quality persisting on into the very term that is reached to-day, and to find, perhaps, in walls of steel and concrete not so much a final perfection of cunning as a brave little effort to make shift with such means as we have, till the real thing comes. Faulty design, even vulgarity, may have its freakish interest. Some eighteenth-century châteaux in the north of France are only one room thick from back to front, to their apparent magnification, though much to the refrigeration of the occupants. Their avenues, too, may have the trees wider apart at one end than at the other, to gain a false effect of length. The droll little snobs! You really cannot be angry with humbugs so infantine. Caddishness itself, when grown into an antique, becomes a curio rather than an offence. And so some charity may well be practised, to one's own profit, in viewing even those fruits of the fancy of speculative builders, the painty red suburban villas that seem to affect a likeness to ordinary houses lightly shelled with field-guns and then glazed at the holes, so that a little window of a funny shape may be found over the chimney-piece or in a corner of a room. If one of them were to live for a thousand years, how much the people of that age would be amused by seeing it! And why not enjoy that amusement ourselves?

THE BEAUTY OF SHADOW

Mary Webb

" They seated themselves under the shade of this
white thorn, and took their solace."

Old Romance.

SHADOW is one of the easiest to perceive of all
nature's beauties. As one may see the charm of
a profile for the first time when looking at a sil-
houette, so one becomes aware of the perfection
of a natural outline more quickly by seeing it
drawn in one colour. It is much simpler to trace
the fairy fretwork of a mountain ash when it lies
on the grass in shadow than when the eyes are
dazzled by the vivid green and clustering scarlet
of berry and leaf against the sky. It has become
a blue tree on the green canvas of a field. Without shadow things would seem unreal, unbreath-
ing as figures in a dream—flat, unrelieved tapestry
on the walls of the world. With it come reality
and rounded loveliness. It is only the bare
winter tree, the barren heart, that are shadowless.

The colours of shadows vary with climate and
season ; they are mauve on ripe corn, deeply
black on hot, white roads in summer, purple on
ploughlands in sandstone country, silver-grey on
snow. Blue is their prevailing colour, varying
from the sapphire of Love-in-a-mist to the indigo
at the root of a thundercloud.

In motion as well as in tint these astral bodies of material things have an ever-changing individuality—faithfully following or waiting beside their prototypes. They flit with the birds, small winged spirits, and even a bee's wing, so unsubstantial itself, has a faint replica that follows its airy fanning. The shade of a leaf caresses its own flower and its fellow-leaf with gentle strokings ; and when a cherry blossom falls down the chequered steeps of the tree, a little mournful shadow goes with her. The shade of the tendrilled creeper steals into a room and lies along the floor, an emissary from the plant outside that peers in but cannot enter. The somnolent gloom thrown by the massed foliage gives majesty to the summer field ; and how splendid, on some loud day in the equinox, is the sight of the dumb shadows of the shouting, gesticulating trees, tossing and bending, lengthening and shrinking over the land. Cloud-shadows on a plain are inexpressibly alluring. Some are like a mere breath on a mirror ; others are dark and ominous, passing into the distance only to be replaced by fresh phalanxes, as though some conquering army had gone forth. But they are most stately over mountains, for they alone have power to darken the everlasting summits.

Midday, the period of practicality, is fitly unshadowed ; perhaps that is why it has so little glamour. But when the tired labourer turns homeward in the evening, he is led or followed by a lengthening shade ; every tree and hedge sends forth a little mimic to join the ranks ; the sheep and cattle walk the fields with shapes of primeval beasts behind them ; houses stand half-circled in black moats ; the world is barred with gold and purple. Now beside the runlets on the hills the pipkins of the mimulus, which have stood half full of shadow all day, brim over. Now the sharp, clear outline of the western hill steadily ascends its neighbour, till all the heather has been quenched except the one line of blood-red at the summit ; the thick curtain covers that also, but it has no power over the immortal heavens. Then comes sleep, and deepens down the world. Out of shadow comes the dewy morning ; into it retires the silent dusk. Out of it, one by one, we wander, our young eyes full of mystery ; into it we all depart, when the noonday heat is past and the labourer turns home.

If you will go out on some June morning, before the earliest bee comes droning by, when the stripes of sunrise lie right across the awakening earth, you will know the fascination of shadows. On such a day they are almost as blue as chicory. As a child, I remember standing awe-stricken at the strange beauty of a well-known field in the magic of a June dawn. It had a line of tall trees in its eastern hedge, and if you watched while the sun rose, you saw what had been a wide, grey expanse suddenly spanned by swart, prostrate giants. It was as if, with one movement, every tree had flung itself upon its face—Mohammedan-wise—at the muezzin of sunrise. Perhaps the memory of such fresh delights, like dew in the flower-cup of life, may linger even after the flower is gathered. Quite early on a summer morning, if you look down an ugly street in a busy town, you will scarcely know it. The rows of houses have ceased to look dull, and have become the opposing

---

vering in the water, flinging largess of money into the vistaed gold of its The sun makes each leaf transparent, whole picture is ardent as the face of el of a flaming star. As the spirit gather some of the beauty, it longs to ite, less bounded ; it desires an infinite which to reflect universal loveliness. the sun and the wind are abroad to-atch the cloud-reflections hurrying along current of a river, or travelling up-stream. is like the striving of two wills for the ; the froth of the current and the foam ouds continually cross.

ssy lakes the surrounding woods meet in hs of the water, and make a strange, new No wonder there are so many legends of and churches under meres, and bells eerily below the water-lilies. Looking nto the limpid quiet, where everything is iar, yet so alien, the eye sees, beyond those ous green glades, habitations of the water-y, twisted of chimney as an elfin chateau, replicas of some cottage on the bank, ng in outline and impossible in perspective. t one can see the inhabitants passing at the the glades, or a white hand waving from ndow of an unsubstantial dwelling. Almost n see the gleaming arm of some water-n—Aigle or Vivian of the Lake—beckoning, and beautiful, or clad in shining samite. gh there is no Hylas now to be charmed into een silence, no Excalibur to be lifted above ere, yet there is still magic in these reflections calm, hot days, water sends up over ban camps of light and darkness ; the street is a tessellated pavement of blue and yellow ; the bush that looks so pathetically inadequate by day throws quite a forest of obscurity and becomes mysterious.

The shadow of a tree upon any house blesses it, weaving with its cool, hypnotic gestures a soothing quiet ; but the place, of all human habitations, where it best loves to linger, is a village street. There each life is framed in garden and orchard ; companies of spirit-shapes go trembling up and down the humble walls and roofs all day from the multitude of surrounding leaves ; in the highway the sunshine sleeps by the shadow of an ivied wall—disturbed only once in an hour, and then simply turning in its sleep. If those other shades, the troubles of life, have become too dense and shouldered out the light, so that the sick imagination sees them as crouching beasts of prey, a pilgrimage to such a tranquil place in lilac time may help to set things right again. In that sequestered road, where the whirr of a linnet's flight is startling, before the first workman comes through the dew, you can hardly fail to gather some share of peace. There, where the wet lilacs fling their fragrance from garden to garden like bridges, and the pale images of their massed blossom and heart-shaped leaves lie all along the way, questionings will seem a little unimportant—the shade-strewn road preaches so sweetly the necessity of interspersed dimness and light. By-and-by a door opens, and a labourer goes whistling down the chequered track that is so like his life. Here, even death loses some of its grimness—its hideousness of association, which is so unnecessary. For

the imaginatio
existence where
flecked with sha
of the Tree of L
that we have con
tree's mysterious

The slightly b
water-shadows—a
if water were a br
they lose in stre
motion of the curre
Were ever forget-n
that gaze skyward
know all the sweetn
until you saw them
spell lies on rivers
them and transfuse t
depths of swaying le
centre, where the ove
sky, very dark at th
banks are steep and
beauty brings the long
some minds) to be abs
in it even to the losing
the person who most ne
ness physically is a boy
pool in the early morning
came near it, with th
melting into laurels or
after death. Beside a full
this longing is strong and
a curve, you stop with a
breath, dazzled by a blaze
on the bank and there lies
beaten gold, gently mov

gently qui
its yellow
reflection.
and the
some ang
strives to
be less fi
future in

When
gether, w
with the
This last
mastery
of the cl

In gla
the dept
world.
villages
ringing
down i
so fami
myster
countr
blurre
waveri
Almos
end of
the wi
one c
maide
bare
Thou
the g
the m
On

and tree vacillating, shimmering patterns that waver to the tree-top and back again, like flocks of hovering golden birds. Far within clear water dwells the sun's twin brother ; there the pale sister of the moon goes sailing ; there the stars glimmer, spreading into little moons, shrinking into mere points of light at the will of the water.

When we look down into the blueness of some little pool, rejoicing in the birdlike passage of the clouds, and then look up to the wide sky, we realize that the finite is like a lake which, as far as its capacity allows, mirrors the infinite ; and when we see the foreshortened image of a poplar stretched in pale colouring beneath it, we have a sudden vision of time as the faint, straitened shadow of eternity.

PHOTOGRAPHS

J. B. Priestley

" I WOULD also recommend," said the late Sir
Walter Raleigh, talking of the Press, " that a
photograph of the author be placed at the head
of every article. I have been saved from many
bad novels by the helpful pictorial advertisements
of modern publishers." I delight in that remark
just as I delight in its author (who has, I maintain,
written the best letters of this century), but I hope
there are not many of his way of thinking. If
we are to be judged now by our photographs,
there are some of us who will have to cast about
for some other way of earning a living, for it is
certain that writing will not keep us. To be
judged by appearances, so long as what are called
good looks are not demanded, does not alarm me.
Anyhow, we all judge in this way daylong and
cannot help it. But actual appearances give a
man a chance ; there are the gleams and glints
in the eye, the play of wrinkles, the antics of
the mouth, all claiming attention ; and there is
always something appealing about a rugged or
vivacious ugliness. A photograph is another
matter. I have never seen a photograph of anybody that made me want to know the person
caught grinning or scowling or gaping in it, for

the camera has a trick of making humanity look either repulsive or insipid, except when it turns us into absolutely comic grotesques as remote from ordinary men and women as the figures of a Punch and Judy show. Consider the creatures who stare at us from the yellowed pages of the family albums. They are, it is true, old-fashioned and somewhat fantastic as to hair and whiskers and cravats, but then so are the people of the drawings of the period, and yet the strangest creatures we see above the signatures of Leech and Keene and du Maurier seem merely odd neighbours when compared with the monsters we see in the albums.

The worst drawing we have ever seen of ourselves, if we exclude the odd scribbles of people whose hand and eye are definitely alienated, has something in it that makes it preferable to the best photograph. Behind the camera there is no memory of how our faces move, and it can only see us as a momentary grouping of light and shadow. The artist is looking before and after as he sets down his portrait, and so he achieves, even in the sketchiest black-and-white, some suggestion of mobility and warmth. In the photograph everything is frozen. If the camera works quickly, as in a snapshot, our appearance during one fleeting moment is caught and fixed, with the result that it shows us something our eyes have never really seen. We are trapped with an insane grin on our faces, it may be, or pinned against the background for ever in a monstrous attitude in which we could not possibly remain for more than two seconds. If the camera works slowly, moving along with time a little way, then we are asked to freeze ourselves. It is true we are generally told to " look natural," but it is obviously impossible to look natural in such circumstances. Long before the two minutes have passed, the beautiful smile we put on has hardened into a ghastly grimace ; we screw up our eyes to protect them from the glare of the lights ; we can feel the veins beginning to stand out in our foreheads ; and we know only too well that we are busy staging a burlesque of ourselves. The camera we confront on these occasions does its work very efficiently, recording with cruel precision every line and shadow of the idiotic face we have put on, a face that is a complete stranger to us.

I do not know which I dislike the more, these set " portraits " or " studies," the work of gentlemen with large studios and temperaments and cameras as big as packing cases, or the " snaps " as some people, in their foul fashion, call them, those fantastic glimpses of oneself standing on the lawn or sitting in a deck-chair, gaping at nothing. More than once, when friends have been showing me photographs of groups of people, I have suddenly caught sight of a face that seemed strange to me, a face singularly vacuous or repulsive, and I have been on the point of crying out : " Who on earth is that ? " when it has dawned upon me sickeningly that that face was my own. I have never imagined myself to be a handsome man, and have even admitted, under pressure, that I am a trifle on the ugly side. But I have examined such snapshots, casual glimpses fixed for ever, with wonder darkening into despair. Surely, I told myself, I

THE BEAUTY OF SHADOW

circled in black moats ; the world is barred with
gold and purple. Now beside the runlets on the
hills the pipkins of the mimulus, which have stood
half full of shadow all day, brim over. Now the
sharp, clear outline of the western hill steadily
ascends its neighbour, till all the heather has been
quenched except the one line of blood-red at the
summit ; the thick curtain covers that also, but
it has no power over the immortal heavens. Then
comes sleep, and deepens down the world. Out
of shadow comes the dewy morning ; into it
retires the silent dusk. Out of it, one by one,
we wander, our young eyes full of mystery ; into
it we all depart, when the noonday heat is past
and the labourer turns home.

If you will go out on some June morning,
before the earliest bee comes droning by, when
the stripes of sunrise lie right across the awakening
earth, you will know the fascination of shadows.
On such a day they are almost as blue as chicory.
As a child, I remember standing awe-stricken at
the strange beauty of a well-known field in the
magic of a June dawn. It had a line of tall trees
in its eastern hedge, and if you watched while the
sun rose, you saw what had been a wide, grey
expanse suddenly spanned by swart, prostrate
giants. It was as if, with one movement, every
tree had flung itself upon its face—Mohammedan-
wise—at the muezzin of sunrise. Perhaps the
memory of such fresh delights, like dew in the
flower-cup of life, may linger even after the flower
is gathered. Quite early on a summer morning, if
you look down an ugly street in a busy town, you
will scarcely know it. The rows of houses have
ceased to look dull, and have become the opposing

79

camps of light and darkness ; the street is a tessellated pavement of blue and yellow ; the bush
that looks so pathetically inadequate by day
throws quite a forest of obscurity and becomes
mysterious.

The shadow of a tree upon any house blesses it,
weaving with its cool, hypnotic gestures a soothing
quiet ; but the place, of all human habitations,
where it best loves to linger, is a village street.
There each life is framed in garden and orchard ;
companies of spirit-shapes go trembling up and
down the humble walls and roofs all day from the
multitude of surrounding leaves ; in the highway
the sunshine sleeps by the shadow of an ivied
wall—disturbed only once in an hour, and then
simply turning in its sleep.   If those other shades,
the troubles of life, have become too dense and
shouldered out the light, so that the sick imagination sees them as crouching beasts of prey, a pilgrimage to such a tranquil place in lilac time may
help to set things right again.   In that sequestered
road, where the whirr of a linnet's flight is startling, before the first workman comes through the
dew, you can hardly fail to gather some share of
peace.   There, where the wet lilacs fling their
fragrance from garden to garden like bridges, and
the pale images of their massed blossom and heart-
shaped leaves lie all along the way, questionings
will seem a little unimportant—the shade-strewn
road preaches so sweetly the necessity of interspersed dimness and light.   By-and-by a door
opens, and a labourer goes whistling down the
chequered track that is so like his life.   Here,
even death loses some of its grimness—its hideousness of association, which is so unnecessary.   For

the imagination sees the highway of mortal existence where it ends abruptly, penumbrous, flecked with shade from the heart-shaped leaves of the Tree of Life : and the shadow is the sign that we have come at last within the pale of the tree's mysterious whisperings.

The slightly blurred colours of reflections—water-shadows—are more vivid than reality, as if water were a brighter medium than air ; what they lose in strength of outline through the motion of the current, they gain in dreamy charm. Were ever forget-me-nots half so blue as those that gaze skyward from clear water ? Did you know all the sweetness of flushed wild-rose faces until you saw them sleeping in a stream ? Some spell lies on rivers where willows bend over them and transfuse them with tender green, with depths of swaying leaf-reflections, lighter in the centre, where the overhanging tracery shows the sky, very dark at the sides, where the grassy banks are steep and the leaves thick. Such beauty brings the longing (almost a torment to some minds) to be absorbed in nature, dissolved in it even to the losing of personality. Perhaps the person who most nearly approaches this one-ness physically is a boy who plunges into a green pool in the early morning. Spiritually, the Greeks came near it, with their legends of maidens melting into laurels or becoming nightingales after death. Beside a full-flowing river in autumn this longing is strong and urgent. Coming round a curve, you stop with a sudden intake of the breath, dazzled by a blaze of glory. There stands on the bank and there lies in the flood a tree of beaten gold, gently moving against the sky, gently quivering in the water, flinging largess of its yellow money into the vistaed gold of its reflection. The sun makes each leaf transparent, and the whole picture is ardent as the face of some angel of a flaming star. As the spirit strives to gather some of the beauty, it longs to be less finite, less bounded ; it desires an infinite future in which to reflect universal loveliness.

When the sun and the wind are abroad together, watch the cloud-reflections hurrying along with the current of a river, or travelling up-stream. This last is like the striving of two wills for the mastery ; the froth of the current and the foam of the clouds continually cross.

In glassy lakes the surrounding woods meet in the depths of the water, and make a strange, new world. No wonder there are so many legends of villages and churches under meres, and bells ringing eerily below the water-lilies. Looking down into the limpid quiet, where everything is so familiar, yet so alien, the eye sees, beyond those mysterious green glades, habitations of the water-country, twisted of chimney as an elfin chateau, blurred replicas of some cottage on the bank, wavering in outline and impossible in perspective. Almost one can see the inhabitants passing at the end of the glades, or a white hand waving from the window of an unsubstantial dwelling. Almost one can see the gleaming arm of some water-maiden—Aigle or Vivian of the Lake—beckoning, bare and beautiful, or clad in shining samite. Though there is no Hylas now to be charmed into the green silence, no Excalibur to be lifted above the mere, yet there is still magic in these reflections.

On calm, hot days, water sends up over bank

and tree vacillating, shimmering patterns that waver to the tree-top and back again, like flocks of hovering golden birds. Far within clear water dwells the sun's twin brother; there the pale sister of the moon goes sailing; there the stars glimmer, spreading into little moons, shrinking into mere points of light at the will of the water.

When we look down into the blueness of some little pool, rejoicing in the birdlike passage of the clouds, and then look up to the wide sky, we realize that the finite is like a lake which, as far as its capacity allows, mirrors the infinite; and when we see the foreshortened image of a poplar stretched in pale colouring beneath it, we have a sudden vision of time as the faint, straitened shadow of eternity.

PHOTOGRAPHS

J. B. Priestley

" I WOULD also recommend," said the late Sir
Walter Raleigh, talking of the Press, " that a
photograph of the author be placed at the head
of every article. I have been saved from many
bad novels by the helpful pictorial advertisements
of modern publishers." I delight in that remark
just as I delight in its author (who has, I maintain,
written the best letters of this century), but I hope
there are not many of his way of thinking. If
we are to be judged now by our photographs,
there are some of us who will have to cast about
for some other way of earning a living, for it is
certain that writing will not keep us. To be
judged by appearances, so long as what are called
good looks are not demanded, does not alarm me.
Anyhow, we all judge in this way daylong and
cannot help it. But actual appearances give a
man a chance ; there are the gleams and glints
in the eye, the play of wrinkles, the antics of
the mouth, all claiming attention ; and there is
always something appealing about a rugged or
vivacious ugliness. A photograph is another
matter. I have never seen a photograph of anybody that made me want to know the person
caught grinning or scowling or gaping in it, for

the camera has a trick of making humanity look either repulsive or insipid, except when it turns us into absolutely comic grotesques as remote from ordinary men and women as the figures of a Punch and Judy show. Consider the creatures who stare at us from the yellowed pages of the family albums. They are, it is true, old-fashioned and somewhat fantastic as to hair and whiskers and cravats, but then so are the people of the drawings of the period, and yet the strangest creatures we see above the signatures of Leech and Keene and du Maurier seem merely odd neighbours when compared with the monsters we see in the albums.

The worst drawing we have ever seen of ourselves, if we exclude the odd scribbles of people whose hand and eye are definitely alienated, has something in it that makes it preferable to the best photograph. Behind the camera there is no memory of how our faces move, and it can only see us as a momentary grouping of light and shadow. The artist is looking before and after as he sets down his portrait, and so he achieves, even in the sketchiest black-and-white, some suggestion of mobility and warmth. In the photograph everything is frozen. If the camera works quickly, as in a snapshot, our appearance during one fleeting moment is caught and fixed, with the result that it shows us something our eyes have never really seen. We are trapped with an insane grin on our faces, it may be, or pinned against the background for ever in a monstrous attitude in which we could not possibly remain for more than two seconds. If the camera works slowly, moving along with time a little way, then we are asked to freeze ourselves. It is true we are generally told to " look natural," but it is obviously impossible to look natural in such circumstances. Long before the two minutes have passed, the beautiful smile we put on has hardened into a ghastly grimace ; we screw up our eyes to protect them from the glare of the lights ; we can feel the veins beginning to stand out in our foreheads ; and we know only too well that we are busy staging a burlesque of ourselves. The camera we confront on these occasions does its work very efficiently, recording with cruel precision every line and shadow of the idiotic face we have put on, a face that is a complete stranger to us.

I do not know which I dislike the more, these set " portraits " or " studies," the work of gentlemen with large studios and temperaments and cameras as big as packing cases, or the " snaps " as some people, in their foul fashion, call them, those fantastic glimpses of oneself standing on the lawn or sitting in a deck-chair, gaping at nothing. More than once, when friends have been showing me photographs of groups of people, I have suddenly caught sight of a face that seemed strange to me, a face singularly vacuous or repulsive, and I have been on the point of crying out : " Who on earth is that ? " when it has dawned upon me sickeningly that that face was my own. I have never imagined myself to be a handsome man, and have even admitted, under pressure, that I am a trifle on the ugly side. But I have examined such snapshots, casual glimpses fixed for ever, with wonder darkening into despair. Surely, I told myself, I am not like *that*. Whatever I may have admitted on the subject of appearances, I have contrived to pass, in the secret councils of my mind, a tiny vote of confidence, on the ground that though I may not conform to certain rather absurd standards, nevertheless there is about my face a *something* that would be appreciated by the wise few. But when I have seen myself staring or grinning in those photographs, I have been compelled to take leave of vanity. So this is the thing that thinks itself so important and dreams its dreams and imagines that other people are interested and friendly or even affectionate! This is what people see and talk to and feed and sometimes cherish! For the space of several seconds I am humility itself.

I fare no better when the camera is leisurely in the " portraits " and " studies." About once a month some photographer writes to suggest that I should give him a sitting, being anxious, he usually writes, to add yet another to his series of portraits or studies of celebrities. And let me say now that I cannot understand why these photographers (Court Photographers, too, some of them) should want my face. I am clearly no beauty, so that no editor of an illustrated weekly wants me to smirk at his readers. I am so remote from any sort of fashionable world that I should never be allowed to pose even as a friend : Lady Woolworth, Mrs. Revoke, Captain Bilker, and Friend ; not even as that. As for being a celebrity, it is absurd ; I am not yet even one of your tiny little lions, roaring you as gently as any sucking dove ; I am merely one of those young men in baggy tweed suits who grumble to other young men in baggy tweed suits that their books do not sell, and are for ever telling one another that other young men still, whose books do sell and whose suits do not bag, are charlatans. For my own part, I should prefer the photograph of any decent bull-terrier. However, such is the fact ; I am asked for a sitting ; and the further fact is that I do not give a sitting. But I will confess that in my time I have given three, with intervals between of despair and mounting hope. I do not remember now whether these men called themselves Court Photographers or Press Photographers. All that I do remember is that they foolishly did it for nothing, that they tried to make me feel important, and that they succeeded in making me look like some one else.

The first photographer, very fashionable and obviously an indefatigable toucher-up, was clearly determined that I should be better-looking at all costs. The result was that he produced an elaborate portrait of a man who was obviously advertising a correspondence course in physical culture, and was equally obviously a fraud. It was in this studio that I encountered the female secretary whose opening remark to me was : " Now tell me all about yourself." I wish I had told her that at least I had no intention of advertising a correspondence course in physical culture. Photographer Number Two, who inhabited a gigantic studio full of guitars and shawls and cushions, and who was evidently highbrow, plumped me into a chair and switched on about ten searchlights, and afterwards produced an excellent likeness of a cleverish young Jew, on the make and quite unscrupulous. It took me two years or more to recover from that satanic transformation, but hope revived at last, and I agreed to visit a man who had done capital photographs of some of my fellow-writers, friends of mine. He was hearty and frank, and did not shrink from pointing out to me that a face like mine was hopeless unless it showed the camera a broad grin. So I grinned away, and he dodged in and out of his black cloth. A week afterwards I was shown half a dozen different portraits of a fellow who looked as if he travelled in wines and spirits during the week, and was the life and soul of the West Ham Dog Fancier's Association every week-end, the kind of man who is waggish with barmaids, and who is referred to whenever you hear a new arrival in a bar asking : " Where's Charlie to-night ? " At first I could not understand why my name had been written on the back of all these photographs, so gross was the transformation.

The truth is, there is malice in the camera just as there is in all these clever modern devices. It is as if the gods should overhear our crowing : " Another improvement ! Another short cut ! Another leap forward ! " and then give a nod to one of the company, who then swiftly contrives that there shall be malice in this new thing we have made. Thus there is a sinister cast in the magic mirror we have devised. It is indeed amazing that a visiting friend, merely by pointing a black box at us and making something click, should be able to catch and retain our fleeting images, pluck out one moment from the flux, so that people unborn may possibly see the light and shadow that was on our faces one summer morning. That morning will be very distant then, will have been whirled away farther than Sirius, will indeed be irretrievably lost, yet those people as they glance at the photographs will spend a second or so at our sides and so will have seen Time defeated. But it is all a cheat. The moment to which they will return will not be the moment we knew when we were facing the camera ; the foolish shadows grinning at them from a lost generation will be no true record but a cold libel, only tampering with their thought of us. That demure servant, the camera, will have had the last laugh.

DUKES' EXCURSIONS

Harold Brighouse

BULUNGAN, in Borneo, which is the Sambir of Almayer and Willems and Tom Lingard. . . . " I'm going there," said K., and though he said it in '99, though he is a travelled man of whom I last heard from Sydney, he . . . no, he never went to Carcassonne nor to Sambir, nor nearer to the painted islands than Shanghai. But it happens, because of K., who introduced me to Nina Almayer, that I am a blue-blooded Conradian, an old inhabitant who knows exactly how an aristocrat feels towards a *nouveau riche*. He feels as I feel towards the people who only heard of Conrad when *Chance* made its lucky strike ; in this matter of Conrad, K. and I allowed *Nostromo* as the unique exception to our rule of being fanatical Archipelagoists.

It's odd, but life is odd, that in those days we had before us a better chance than most of going to Malaya. When K. first put *The Outcast* in my hands, scorning triumphant gesture but implying, for all that, that he had discovered a continent, we were apprentices together in a shipping merchant's, in Whitworth Street, Manchester, and already we wore invisible labels, mine, though I was not to know of it till later, the more Conradly of the two. The Private Office in its omniscience mentally stencilled K. " Bombay," and stencilled me " Singapore." But there came a year when, for six months, summer months, the hours were nine till nine, with pay twelve shillings a week and " tea-money " (sixpence, I swear), and one needn't be called an idle apprentice for revolting. I went ; K. stayed ; he, when the East called like a destiny, was not to be deterred by a summer of man's hard labour at boy's wages.

Invincibly romantic were the letters he wrote me from his room in Watson's Hotel, Bombay. Watson's, I seem to remember, was on the site of, or actually reconstructed from, an old John Company fort ; he lived there for three years in the glamour of the past with the glamorous islands in his plotted future. Well, as I say, he saw the China Seas, but from a hurrying liner ; he never went to Sambir nor to Patusan, and now I hear that he is coming home " to settle." Vaguely I thought to beat him in the end. Capriciously the notion came to me that, outward bound for Conrad's islands, I might pass K. somewhere at sea ; but, instead, I shall meet him when he lands. Berkeley Square has squelched my infirm resolution.

Not that I'm habitual in Berkeley Square ; not that I have travelled so far as that from Whitworth Street ; but I have a later friend than K., a curious amphibious creature who swims in society and walks amongst the arts, and when I go to see him in Berkeley Square I meet the aristocrats. I don't dine there. I'm afraid of the butler. But aristocrats take tea, and the butler, it's astonishing to know, has a frailty. When Chelsea play at home he goes to watch them ; therefore I watch the football calendar to learn when I may go with confidence to Berkeley Square.

The aristocrats were speaking of travel, commiserating a poor devil forced by the need to economize to cross the Atlantic on the *Berengaria* without once entering the Ritz-Carlton restaurant. He's been driven to eat table d'hôte in the ordinary dining saloon, with the ruck of the first-class passengers. As he explained, it was either that or a cabin without a private bath. So they cursed taxation, then turned to plans for their wintering. The principle, as far as I could discern one, is that distance lends enchantment. Thus Switzerland is vulgar. A hefty youth tried to argue that some Swiss resort, the name of which I failed to catch, is " still tolerable." " Bobby," a lady declared, " when you see skis you can't see a suburb," and some witticisms ensued—the pronunciation, you know, of the word " ski "— which seemed to me hardly worthy of Berkeley Square. But there ! We simple-minded others are always having our illusions shattered ; it occasioned me a moment of surprise to find that, though Switzerland was vulgar, Florida was not. The surprise arose out of personal experience, not of Florida but of Southern California, which, after all, was the American Riviera until they did things to the drainage system and to the mosquitoes of the Florida swamps. My point about California is that it is lovely, even its desert, except for the gross vulgarization of its bathing-beaches, and I apprehended the same of Florida. I'm wrong, of course ; Berkeley Square is going

to Florida ; a jazz band in Mürren is vulgar, but
one in Miami isn't (which may be very true ;
vulgarity is the obtrusion of the inappropriate),
because Berkeley Square decrees. All the same,
the Floridans were not allowed to score too
highly ; they were told that they'd be depending
on hotels. The others were going to Gussie's,
and there was a new motor road by which it was
only two hundred miles to Eleanor's, and after
that one pushed out to the big-game country.
Gussie, it appears, makes two coffee beans grow
where there were none before, and Eleanor's cove
(=husband) has a ranch, and if there was once
a bit of trouble out there in Kenya—something
about some East Indians with too literal ideas
of Empire citizenship—all that is over now, and
Kenya (I gathered) has been made safe for
aristocracy, a modern edition of old Virginia.
Anyhow, Kenya wasn't trippery, like—oh, they
were aristocrats, they tolerated the ski fanatic—
like Egypt, they tactfully compared. And finally
there was a woman who was going alone to Rio.
" Might as well look at that harbour," she offered
as a motive. Finally ? And there was I, and
Bulungan in Borneo seemed to me just then a
good mine to spring. Far-flung as they proposed
to be, nobody, I thought, approached my aspira-
tion of the Archipelago.

Nicely, they brought me into it ; generously
they seemed to take it for granted that I, too,
would be wintering abroad ; they asked my plans,
and I said I contemplated Borneo. Probably I
said it with a certain pride. " Oh, yes ! " And
the condescension, if unstressed, was evident.
" Bertie, when was it we went to Sarawak to see

them all ? Four years ago ? " Was that it ?
Was I four years behind the fashion ? But they
couldn't have thought of . . . the lady went on.
" When," she reminded Bertie, " Monty's yacht
came out to meet us, and we did the round of the
Conrad Harbours."

Just like that ! The round of the Conrad
Harbours ! Or, if I went to Patusan there'd be
an esplanade and a first-class hotel, and a band
playing " The Karain Crawl." And I can't
afford it, anyhow ; it's a mistake to have an
amphibious friend, or if one has him to visit him
in the wrong of his two elements. I shall read
Almayer again, the fifteenth time. Two pages
of *Almayer* will give me back my Sambir as it is
and always will be. Amen.

(From the *Manchester Guardian*.)

CATS

Robert Lynd

The Champion Cat Show has been held at the Crystal Palace, but the champion cat was not there. One could not possibly allow him to appear in public. He is for show, but not in a cage. He does not compete, because he is above competition. You know this as well as I. Probably you possess him. I certainly do. That is the supreme test of a cat's excellence—the test of possession. One does not say : " You should see Brailsford's cat," or " You should see Adcock's cat," or " You should see Sharp's cat," but " You should see our cat." There is nothing we are more egoistic about—not even children— than about cats. I have heard a man, for lack of anything better to boast about, boasting that his cat eats cheese. In any one else's cat it would have seemed an inferior habit, and only worth mentioning to the servant as a warning. But because the cat happens to be his cat, this man talks about its vice excitedly among women as though it were an accomplishment. It is seldom that we hear a cat publicly reproached with guilt by any one above a cook. He is not permitted to steal from our own larder. But if he visits the next-door house by stealth and returns over the wall with a Dover sole in his jaws, we really cannot help laughing. We are a little nervous at first, and our mirth is tinged with pity at the thought of the probably elderly and dyspeptic gentleman who has had his luncheon filched away almost from under his nose. If we were quite sure that it was from No. 14 and not from No. 9 or No. 11 that the fish had been stolen, we might—conceivably—call round and offer to pay for it. But with a cat one is never quite sure. And we cannot call round on all the neighbours and make a general announcement that our cat is a thief. In any case, the next move lies with the wronged neighbour. As day follows day, and there is no sign of his irate and murder-bent figure advancing up the path, we recover our mental balance and begin to see the cat's exploit in a new light. We do not yet extol it on moral grounds, but undoubtedly, the more we think of it, the deeper becomes our admiration. Of the two great heroes of the Greeks we admire one for his valour and one for his cunning. The epic of the cat is the epic of Odysseus. The old gentleman with the Dover sole gradually assumes the aspect of a Polyphemus outwitted and humiliated to the point of not even being able to throw things after his tormentor. Clever cat! Nobody else's cat could have done such a thing. We should like to celebrate the Rape of the Dover Sole in Latin verse.

As for the Achillean sort of prowess, we do not demand it of a cat, but we are proud of it when it exists. There is a pleasure in seeing strange cats fly at his approach, either in single file over the wall or in the scattered aimlessness of a bursting bomb. Theoretically, we hate him to fight, but, if he does fight and comes home with a torn ear, we have to summon up all the resources of our finer nature in order not to rejoice on noticing that the cat next door looks as though it had been through a railway accident. I am sorry for the cat next door. I hate him so, and it must be horrible to be hated. But he should not sit on my wall and look at me with yellow eyes. If his eyes were any other colour—even the blue that is now said to be the mark of the runaway husband—I feel certain I could just manage to endure him. But they are the sort of yellow eyes that you expect to see looking out at you from a hole in the panelling in a novel by Mr. Sax Rohmer. The only reason why I am not frightened of them is that the cat is so obviously frightened of me. I never did him any injury, unless to hate is to injure. But he lowers his head when I appear as though he expected to be guillotined. He does not run away : he merely crouches like a guilty thing. Perhaps he remembers how often he has stepped delicately over my seed-beds, but not so delicately as to leave no mark of ruin among the infant lettuces and the less-than-infant autumn-sprouting broccoli. These things I could forgive him, but it is not easy to forgive him the look in his eyes when he watches a bird at its song. They are ablaze with evil. He becomes a sort of Jack the Ripper at the opera. People tell us that we should not blame cats for this sort of thing—that it is their nature and so forth. They even suggest that a cat is no more cruel in eating robin than we are cruel ourselves in eating chicken. This seems to me to be quibbling. In the first place, there is an immense difference between a robin and a chicken. In the second place, we are willing to share our chicken with the cat—at least, we are willing to share the skin and such of the bones as are not required for soup. Besides, a cat has not the same need of delicacies as a human being. It can eat, and even digest, anything. It can eat the black skin of filleted plaice. It can eat the bits of gristle that people leave on the side of their plates. It can eat boiled cod. It can eat New Zealand mutton. There is no reason why an animal with so undiscriminating a palate should demand song-birds for its food, when even human beings, who are fairly unscrupulous eaters, have agreed in some measure to abstain from them. On reflection, however, I doubt if it is his appetite for birds that makes the cat with the yellow eyes feel guilty. If you were able to talk to him in his own language, and formulate your accusations against him as a bird-eater, he would probably be merely puzzled and look on you as a crank. If you pursued the argument and compelled him to moralize his position, he would, I fancy, explain that the birds were very wicked creatures, and that their cruelties to the worms and the insects were more than flesh and blood could stand. He would work himself up into a generous idealization of himself as the guardian of law and order amid the bloody strife of the cabbage-patch— the preserver of the balance of nature. If cats were as clever as we, they would compile an atrocities blue-book about worms. Alas, poor thrush, with how bedraggled a reputation you would come through such an exposure! With how Hunnish a tread you would be depicted treading the lawn, sparing neither age nor sex, seizing the infant worm as it puts out its head to take its first bewildered peep at the rolling sun! Cats could write sonnets on such a theme. . . . Then there is that other beautiful potential poem, " The Cry of the Snail." . . . How tender-hearted cats are! Their sympathy seems to be all but universal, always on the look-out for an object, ready to extend itself anywhere where it is needed, except, as is but human, to their victims. Yellow eyes or not, I begin to be persuaded that the cat next door is a noble fellow. It may well be that his look as I pass is a look not of fear but of repulsion. He has seen me going out among the worms with a sharp—no, not a very sharp—spade, and regards me as no better than an ogre. If I could only explain to him! But I shall never be able to do so. He could no more appreciate my point of view about worms than I can appreciate his about robins. Luckily, we both eat chicken. This may ultimately help us to understand one another.

On the other hand, part of the fascination of cats may be due to the fact that it is so difficult to come to an understanding with them. A man talks to a horse or a dog as to an equal. To a cat he has to be deferential as though it had some Sphinx-like quality that baffled him. He cannot order a cat about with the certainty of being obeyed. He cannot be sure that, if he speaks to it, it will even raise its eyes. If it is perfectly comfortable, it will not. A cat is obedient only when it is hungry or when it takes the fancy.

It may be a parasite, but it is never a servant. The dog does your bidding, but you do the cat's. At the same time, the contrast between the cat and the dog has often been exaggerated by dog-lovers. They tell you stories of dogs that remained with their dead masters, as though there were no fidelity in cats. It was only the other day, however, that the newspapers gave an account of a cat that remained with the body of its murdered mistress in the most faithful tradition of the dogs. I know, again, of cats that will go out for a walk with a human fellow-creature, as dogs do. I have frequently seen a lady walking across Hampstead Heath with a cat in train. When you go for a walk with a dog, however, the dog protects you ; when you go for a walk with a cat, you feel that you are protecting the cat. It is strange that the cat should have imposed the myth of its helplessness on us. It is an animal with an almost boundless capacity for self-help. It can jump up walls. It can climb trees. It can run, as the proverb says, like " greased lightning." It is armed like an African chief. Yet it has contrived to make itself a pampered pet, so that we are alarmed if it attempts to follow us out of the gate into a world of dogs, and only feel happy when it is purring—rolling on its back and purring as we rub its Adam's apple—by the fireside. There is nothing that gives a greater sense of comfort than the purring of a cat. It is the most flattering music in nature. One feels, as one listens, like a humble lover in a bad novel, who says : " You do, then, like me—a little—after all ? " The fact that a cat is not utterly miserable in our presence always comes with the freshness and delight of a surprise. The happiness of a crowing baby, newly introduced to us, may be still more flattering, but a cat will get round people who cannot tolerate babies.

It is all the more to be wondered at that a cat, which is such a master of this conversational sort of music, should ever attempt any other. There never was an animal less fit to be a singer. Some one—was it Cowper?—has said that there are no really ugly voices in nature, and that he could imagine that there was something to be said even for the donkey's bray. I should have thought that the beautiful voices in nature were few, and that most of them could be defended only on the ground of some pleasant association. Humanity, at least, has been unanimous in its condemnation of the cat as part of nature's chorus. Poems have been written in praise of the corncrake as a singer, but never of the cat. All the associations we have with cats have not accustomed us to that discordant howl. It converts love itself into a torment such as can be found only in the pages of a twentieth-century novel. In it we hear the jungle decadent—the beast in dissolution, but not yet civilized. When it rises at night outside the window, we always explain to visitors: " No ; that's not Peter. That's the cat next door with the yellow eyes." The man who will not defend the honour of his cat cannot be trusted to defend anything.

THE ACHIEVEMENT OF THE CAT

" Saki " (H. H. Munro)

IN the political history of nations it is no un-common experience to find States and peoples which but a short time since were in bitter con-flict and animosity with each other, settled down comfortably on terms of mutual goodwill and even alliance. The natural history of the social developments of species affords a similar instance in the coming - together of two once warring elements, now represented by civilized man and the domestic cat. The fiercely waged struggle which went on between humans and felines in those far-off days when sabre-toothed tiger and cave lion contended with primeval man, has long ago been decided in favour of the most fitly equipped combatant—the Thing with a Thumb— and the descendants of the dispossessed family are relegated to-day, for the most part, to the waste lands of jungle and veld, where an existence of self-effacement is the only alternative to ex-termination. But the *felis catus*, or whatever species was the ancestor of the modern domestic cat (a vexed question at present), by a master-stroke of adaptation avoided the ruin of its race, and " captured " a place in the very keystone of the conqueror's organization. For not as a bond-servant or dependent has this proudest of mammals entered the human fraternity; not as a slave like the beasts of burden, or a humble camp-follower like the dog. The cat is domestic only as far as suits its own ends; it will not be kennelled or harnessed, nor suffer any dictation as to its goings out or comings in. Long contact with the human race has developed in it the art of diplomacy, and no Roman cardinal of mediæval days knew better how to ingratiate himself with his surroundings than a cat with a saucer of cream on its mental horizon. But the social smoothness, the purring innocence, the softness of the velvet paw may be laid aside at a moment's notice, and the sinuous feline may disappear, in deliberate aloofness, to a world of roofs and chimney-stacks, where the human element is distanced and disregarded. Or the innate savage spirit that helped its survival in the bygone days of tooth and claw may be summoned forth from beneath the sleek exterior, and the torture-instinct (common alone to human and feline) may find free play in the death-throes of some luckless bird or rodent. It is, indeed, no small triumph to have combined the untrammelled liberty of primeval savagery with the luxury which only a highly developed civilization can command; to be lapped in the soft stuffs that commerce has gathered from the far ends of the world; to bask in the warmth that labour and industry have dragged from the bowels of the earth; to banquet on the dainties that wealth has bespoken for its table, and withal to be a free son of nature, a mighty hunter, a spiller of life-blood. This is the victory of the cat. But besides the credit of success the cat has other qualities which compel recognition. The animal which the Egyptians worshipped as divine, which the Romans venerated as a symbol of liberty, which Europeans in the ignorant Middle Ages anathematized as an agent of demonology, has displayed to all ages two closely-blended characteristics—courage and self-respect. No matter how unfavourable the circumstances, both qualities are always to the fore. Confront a child, a puppy, and a kitten with a sudden danger ; the child will turn instinctively for assistance, the puppy will grovel in abject submission to the impending visitation, the kitten will brace its tiny body for a frantic resistance. And disassociate the luxury-loving cat from the atmosphere of social comfort in which it usually contrives to move, and observe it critically under the adverse conditions of civilization—that civilization which can impel a man to the degradation of clothing himself in tawdry ribald garments and capering mountebank dances in the streets for the earning of the few coins that keep him on the respectable, or non-criminal, side of society. The cat of the slums and alleys—starved, outcast, harried, still keeps amid the prowlings of its adversity the bold, free, panther-tread with which it paced of yore the temple courts of Thebes, still displays the self-reliant watchfulness which man has never taught it to lay aside. And when its shifts and clever managings have not sufficed to stave off inexorable fate, when its enemies have proved too strong or too many for its defensive powers, it dies fighting to the last, quivering with the choking rage of mastered re-

sistance, and voicing in its death-yell that agony
of bitter remonstrance which human animals, too,
have flung at the powers that may be ; the last
protest against a destiny that might have made
them happy—and has not.

NINE LIVES

"The Londoner"

BEING, at this moment, something out of humour with life, I envy most my cat. Of all my friends, she is the wisest. She is sixty miles away from where I sit here writing. Yet I know well how it is with her. That little half-hour of sun had found her stretched out upon a wicker-work seat under the old vine that is southward of my house. Her fur was warm in it and keeps yet the warmth.

She is content. They have brought her milk and she has lapped it slowly, tasting it with each lap of the tongue, not hastening as do cats that are houseless and without service. After this breaking of the fast she has washed herself from ears to tail, deliberately, with nice ceremony, like a priestess who must go clean of body to the holy rites. And then, I know, she took the sun and eased every limb in that mild light. Her yellow eyes blink ; she is deep in comfortable meditation. She is very wise, but not in our troublesome wisdom. For in the passing of her nine lives she learns how to live.

That every pussy has nine lives is a truth not to be questioned. I have never doubted it, although it be a hard saying and mysterious. For if you tell the cat's years as we number our own, pussy's life seems but a span-long life, very short and soon to pass. It is not well with us who love to have the most companionable of all the beasts near to us for sympathy. They go but a little way with us and then leave us. It is not good for us to measure life by the deaths of so many friends ; I am not yet comforted for the death of the pussy who, when I wrote, loved to keep very near to me, lying across my shoulders.

And yet, though in the sight of men they seem to hasten away, the truth is in that old wisdom. We have but one life and they have nine, a taste of the leisures of immortality. I think that in their short years they live out the nine—serenely, graciously, without care and hastening. Care, says the proverb, once killed a cat. It may be so, but it has killed never another.

Pussy was a goddess in old Egypt, and she has never forgotten it. Old incense perfumes her soft fur. A goddess in exile, she exacts honour as any queen who has lost a realm but will have her court and its courtesies. Obedience is strange to her. All the tribe of dog may be at your command ; pussy-cat must not be commanded, but entreated. For this I love her and company with her, not loving to have any but an equal near me in the privacy of my room. We are of the same mood, she and I.

We lie under the same condemnation. We have the same liking for long leisure, the meditative humour ; and there are those who will call us lazy in the grain of us. We are both inapt for any toil, although I, who am under the curse of Adam, who am not of the divine stock, must sadly labour for the pair of us and for the bread of all those who in my house do service and worship to the cat.

There is a foolish legend that the catching of mice is a cat's duty, her share of the world's work. It is true that she catches them ; one was brought to me yesterday and dropped on the hearthrug by a cat who has a sportsmanlike vanity and would be praised and called a hunting Diana. But this is not work ; the census-taker does not put the slayer of pheasants beside the bricklayer and the journalist, as a toiler among the toilers. A saddle for the horse and a collar for the house-dog. If the cat wait long hours, silent beside the crack of the wainscot, it is for pure pleasure. Cats do not keep the mice away ; it is my belief that they preserve them for the chase.

She has nine lives because she can spend well the one life that runs between the hour when mewling, blind, she is new-born in a basket, and the hour when she will die, simply and decently, without fear or regret, like a cat. She has warmed all four paws at the fire of life, and, when the time comes, will be ready to depart. All her desires have been fulfilled in living ; the long hours of basking idleness have brought her the last wisdom. Enviously, I think it might be so with me if life were less cumbered with foolish business.

I will compare her with the Buddhist who goes apart from his fellows to meditate upon the Way. But the Buddhist cuts a pitiful figure when you compare him with pussy. He must go out and away and be alone, enduring hardness, before he can begin his thinking. My admirable cat has never denied herself one of the little pleasures of life. She eats delicately, will have her milk of the newest, and tells me, clawing gently at my knee, that she is eager after fish. She will lie soft at night, and, by day, will take the sun as though it shone for her ; she dreams happily by the winter fire. Yet if the Buddhist, in his long meditation, touch at the limit of wisdom and come to that boundary wall which marks the last marches of knowledge, he will find that my cat is there before, is there upon the wall, looking down on him, blinking yellow eyes in pity upon the poor man who has been vexed by his dream of life beyond life in wearisome reincarnations. She knows that nine lives are enough, and that sleep is good.

ON THEM

Hilaire Belloc

I DO not like Them. It is no good asking me why, though I have plenty of reasons. I do not like Them. There would be no particular point in saying I do not like Them if it were not that so many people doted on Them, and when one hears Them praised, it goads one to expressing one's hatred and fear of Them.

I know very well that They can do one harm, and that They have occult powers. All the world has known that for a hundred thousand years, more or less, and every attempt has been made to propitiate Them. James I. would drown Their mistress or burn her, but *They* were spared. Men would mummify them in Egypt, and worship the mummies; men would carve Them in stone in Cyprus, and Crete and Asia Minor, or (more remarkable still) artists, especially in the Western Empire, would leave Them out altogether; so much was Their influence dreaded. Well, I yield so far as not to print Their name, and only to call Them " They ", but I hate Them, and I'm not afraid to say so.

If you will take a little list of the chief crimes that living beings can commit you will find that They commit them all. And They are

cruel ; cruelty is even in Their tread and expression. They are hatefully cruel. I saw one of
Them catch a mouse the other day (the cat is
now out of the bag), and it was a very much more
sickening sight, I fancy, than ordinary murder.
You may imagine that They catch mice to eat
them. It is not so. They catch mice to torture
them. And, what is worse, They will teach this
to Their children—Their children who are naturally innocent and fat, and full of goodness, are
deliberately and systematically corrupted by
Them ; there is diabolism in it.

Other beings (I include mankind) will be gluttonous, but gluttonous spasmodically, or with
a method, or shamefacedly, or, in some way or
another that qualifies the vice ; not so They.
They are gluttonous always and upon all occasions, and in every place and for ever. It was
only last Vigil of All Fools' Day when, myself
fasting, I filled up the saucer seven times with
milk and seven times it was emptied, and there
went up the most peevish, querulous, vicious
complaint and demand for an eighth. They will
eat some part of the food of all that are in the
house. Now even a child, the most gluttonous
one would think of all living creatures, would not
do that. It makes a selection, *They* do not.
They will drink beer. This is not a theory ; I
know it ; I have seen it with my own eyes.
They will eat special foods ; They will even eat
dry bread. Here again I have personal evidence
of the fact ; They will eat the dog's biscuits, but
never upon any occasion will They eat anything
that has been poisoned, so utterly lacking are
They in simplicity and humility, and so abomin-

ably well filled with cunning by whatever demon first brought Their race into existence.

They also, alone of all creation, love hateful noises. Some beings indeed (and I count Man among them) cannot help the voice with which they have been endowed, but they know that it is offensive, and are at pains to make it better ; others (such as the peacock or the elephant) also know that their cry is unpleasant. They therefore use it sparingly. Others again, the dove, the nightingale, the thrush, know that their voices are very pleasant, and entertain us with them all day and all night long ; but They now that Their voices are the most hideous of all the sounds in the world, and, knowing this, They perpetually insist upon thrusting those voices upon us, saying, as it were, " I am giving myself pain, but I am giving you more pain, and therefore I shall go on." And They choose for the place where this pain shall be given, exact and elevated situations, very close to our ears. Is there any need for me to point out that in every city They will begin Their wicked jar just at the time when its inhabitants must sleep ? In London you will not hear it till after midnight ; in the county towns it begins at ten ; in remote villages as early as nine.

Their Master also protects Them. They have a charmed life. I have seen one thrown from a great height into a London street, which when It reached it It walked quietly away with the dignity of the Lost World to which It belonged.

If one had the time one could watch Them day after day, and never see Them do a single kind or good thing, or be moved by a single virtuous impulse. They have no gesture for the expression of admiration, love, reverence, or ecstasy. They have but one method of expressing content, and They reserve that for moments of physical repletion. The tail, which is in all other animals the signal for joy or for defence, or for mere usefulness, or for a noble anger, is with Them agitated only to express a sullen discontent.

All that They do is venomous, and all that They think is evil, and when I take mine away (as I mean to do next week—in a basket), I shall first read in a book of statistics what is the wickedest part of London, and I shall leave It there, for I know of no one even among my neighbours quite so vile as to deserve such a gift.

THE LORD OF LIFE

E. V. Lucas

"What right has that man to have a spaniel?" said a witty lady, pointing to a bully: "spaniels should be a reward."

In his prescription for the perfect home Southey included a little girl rising six years and a kitten rising six weeks. That is perhaps the prettiest thing that ever found its way from his pen—that patient, plodding, bread-winning pen, which he drove with such pathetic industry as long as he had any power left with which to urge it forward. A little girl rising six years and a kitten rising six weeks. Charming, isn't it?

But, my dear rascally Lake Poet, what about a puppy rising six months? How did you come to forget that?—such a puppy as is in this room as I write: a small black puppy of the Cocker spaniel blood, so black that had the good God not given him a gleaming white corner to his wicked little eye, one would not know at dinner whether he was sitting by one's side or not—not, that is, until his piercing shrieks, signifying that he had been (very properly) trodden on again, rent the welkin.

This puppy have I called the Lord of Life because I cannot conceive of a more complete embodiment of vitality, curiosity, success, and tyranny. Vitality first and foremost. It is incredible that so much pulsating quicksilver, so much energy and purpose, should be packed into a foot and a half of black hide. He is up earliest in the morning, he retires last at night. He sleeps in the day, it is true, but it is sleep that hangs by a thread. Let there be a footfall out of place, let a strange dog in the street venture but to breathe a little louder than usual, let the least rattle of plates strike upon his ear, and his sleep is shaken from him in an instant. From an older dog one expects some of this watchfulness. But when an absurd creature of four months with one foot still in the cradle is so charged with vigilance, it is ridiculous.

If nothing occurs to interest him, and his eyes are no longer heavy (heavy ! he never had heavy eyes), he will make drama for himself. He will lay a slipper at your feet and bark for it to be thrown. I admire him most when he is returning with it in his mouth. The burden gives him responsibility : his four black feet, much too big for his body, all move at once with a new importance and rhythm. When he runs for the slipper he is just so much galvanized puppy rioting with life ; when he returns he is an official, a guardian, a trustee ; his eye is grave and responsible ; the conscientious field spaniel wakes in him and asserts itself.

As to his curiosity, it knows no bounds. He must be acquainted with all that happens. What kind of a view of human life a dog, even a big dog, acquires, I have sometimes tried to imagine by kneeling or lying full length on the ground and looking up. The world then becomes strangely incomplete : one sees little but legs. Of course the human eye is set differently in the head, and a dog can visualize humanity without injuring his neck as I must do in that grovelling posture ; but none the less the dog's view of his master standing over him must be very partial, very fragmentary. Yet this little puppy, although his eyes are within eight inches of the ground, gives the impression that he sees all. He goes through the house with a microscope.

But for his dependence, his curiosity, and his proprietary instinct to be studied at their best, you should see him in an empty house. All dogs like to explore empty houses with their masters, but none more than he. His paws never so resound as when they patter over the bare boards of an empty house. He enters each room with the eye of an auctioneer, a builder, tenant, furnisher, and decorator in one. I never saw such comprehensive glances, such a nose for a colour scheme. But leave him by accident behind a closed door and see what happens. Not the mandrake torn bleeding from its earth ever shrieked more melancholy. Yet tears are instant with him always, in spite of his native cheerfulness. It was surely a puppy that inspired the proverb about crying before you are hurt.

I spoke of his success. That is perhaps his most signal characteristic, for the world is at his feet. Whether indoors or out, he has his own way, instantly follows his own inclination. It is one of his most charming traits that he thinks visibly. I often watch him thinking. " Surely it's time tea was brought," I can positively see him saying to himself. " I hope that cake wasn't finished yesterday : it was rather more decent than usual. I believe those girls eat it in the kitchen." Or, " He's putting on his heavy boots : that means the hill. Good ! I'll get near the door so as to be sure of slipping out with him." Or, " It's no good : he's not going for a walk this morning. That stupid old desk again, I suppose." Or, " Who was that ? Oh, only the postman. I shan't bark for him." Or, " I'm getting awfully hungry. I'll go and worry the cook."

But the most visible token of his success is the attention, the homage, he receives from strangers. For he not only dominates the house, but has a procession of admirers after him in the streets. Little girls and middle-aged ladies equally ask permission to pat him. Old gentlemen ask if he is for sale, and inquire his price. Not that he looks valuable—as a matter of fact, though pure he is not remarkable—but that he suggests so much companionship and fun. One recognizes instantly the Vital Spark.

When it comes to the consideration of his tyranny, there enters a heavy spaniel named Bush and a dainty capricious egoist in blue-grey whom we will call Smoke. Smoke once had a short way with dogs ; but the Lord of Life has changed all that. Smoke once would draw back a paw of velvet, dart it forward like the tongue of a serpent and return to sleep again, perfectly secure in her mind that that particular dog would harass her no more. But do you think she ever hurt the puppy in that way ? Never. He loafs into the room with his hands in his pockets and his head full of mischief, perceives a long bushy blue-grey tail hanging over the edge of the sofa, and forthwith gives it such a pull with his teeth as a Siberian householder who had been out late and had lost his latch key might at his door bell when the wolves were after him. An ordinary dog would be blinded for less ; but not so our friend. Smoke merely squeaks reproach, and in a minute or two, when the puppy has tired a little of the game, he is found not only lying beside her and stealing her warmth, but lying in the very centre of the nest in the cushion that she had fashioned for herself. Tyranny, if you like !

And Bush ! Poor Bush. For every spoiled new-comer there is, I suppose, throughout life an old, faithful friend who finds himself on the shelf. It is not quite so bad as this with Bush, and when the puppy grows up and is staid too, Bush will return to his own again ; but I must admit that at the beginning he had a very hard time of it. For the puppy, chiefly by hanging on his ear, first infuriated him into sulks, and then, his mastery being recognized, set to work systematically to tease and bully him. The result is that now Bush actually has to ask permission before he dares to take up his old seat by my chair ; he may have it only if the puppy does not want it.

But Bush is not my theme ; Bush was never a Lord of Life : his pulse was always a little slow, his nature a little too much inclined to accept rather than initiate. Nor, I suppose, will our Lord of Life be quite such a Lord much longer, for with age will come an increase of sobriety, a diminution of joy. That he will not untimely fall by the way, but will grow up to serious spanielhood, I feel as sure as if an angel had forewarned me ; but were he now to die this should be his epitaph : " Here lies a Lord of Life, aged six months. He would never be broken to the house, but after sin was adorable."

THE GREATEST TEST MATCH

Neville Cardus

ON a bright day in the spring of 1921 I went to
Lord's, hoping to see the first practice of the
Australians. But the place was deserted, save
for the man at the gates. He told me Armstrong's
men were being entertained that afternoon somewhere in the City, and that they wouldn't be in
the nets till after tea. Still, he added, with a
touch of human nature not too common at Lord's,
if I liked I could enter the ground and sit and
enjoy myself in the sun till they came.

I sat on a bench with my feet spread out so
that they touched the soft grass. A great calm
was over the field. The trees beyond the
" nursery " were delicate with fresh green, and
the fine old pavilion seemed to nod in the sunshine. It was an occasion for a reverie, and I
fell to affectionate thoughts upon the great days
of cricket, of the history that had been made
on the field which stretched before me. I
thought of Grace, of Spofforth, of Hornby, of
A. G. Steel. . . . Maybe I dozed for a while.
Then I was conscious of a voice. " Would you
mind moving up a little ? This seat is rather
congested." I looked around and saw sitting by
my side a man in a tight black coat which but-
toned high on his chest. He had side whiskers

and wore a low turned-down collar and a high
bowler hat. A handkerchief was showing from
a breast pocket in his jacket. Not quite awake
yet, I "moved up." "Thank you," he said.
"I'm sorry I disturbed you. A nap carries one
comfortably through a long wait at these matches.
What a crowd there is!" I looked round. I
was in the middle of a big crowd indeed. In
front of me sat a parson. He was reading the
Times. I glanced over his shoulder and saw the
headline: "Egyptian Campaign: Sir G. Wolse-
ley's Dispatch." The man at my side said,
"Were you here yesterday, sir?" and before I
could reply he added, "It was a considerable
day's cricket, and the *Post* has an excellent
account. Perhaps you've seen it?" He handed
me a copy of the *Morning Post*, and, thanking
him, I took it. The paper was dated August
29, 1882. In a column headed "England *v.*
Australia" I read that, on the day before,
Australia had been dismissed for 63 by Barlow
and Peate, and that England, captained by A. N.
Hornby, had made, in reply, 101. Then I understood my situation. And what is more I now
understood it without the slightest astonish-
ment. Even the aspect of the ground, which told
me it was Kennington Oval and not Lord's, did
not embarrass me. It was enough that I was
one of the crowd that was to witness the second
day's cricket in the ninth Test match—the most
famous Test match of all.

I gave the *Post* back to my companion in
silence. "A considerable day's cricket indeed,
sir," said the Parson. "But England ought to
have made more runs. Our batting was dis-

tinctly mediocre—almost as bad as the Australians'." A loud cheer disturbed his argument. Down the pavilion steps walked the England Eleven in single file, led by Hornby. With him was W. G., and he passed along the field with an ambling motion, and the wind got into his great black beard. He spoke to Hornby in a high-pitched voice and laughed. Then he threw the ball to a tall, graceful player just behind him and cried, "Catch her, Bunny." Following Grace and Hornby were Lucas, C. T. Studd, J. M. Read, the Hon. A. Lyttelton, Ulyett, Barlow, W. Barnes, A. G. Steel, and Peate. The crowd quietened, awaiting the advent of Australia's first two batsmen, and I again heard the Parson's voice " . . . The English total was distressingly poor. Rarely have I seen poorer batting from an All England Eleven. The fact is, sir, that for some little time now English cricket has been deteriorating. Our batsmen don't hit the ball as hard as they used to do, and even our bowling. . . ." Another cheer drowned his discourse. " Bannerman and Massie," said my companion. " I should imagine Bannerman's the youngest man in the match." The Parson was prompt with his correction. " I believe S. P. Jones, who was twenty-one on the 1st of the month, is the junior member of the two teams. Studd is, I fancy, eleven months older than Jones. Bannerman is twenty-three at least, and Giffen is six days younger than Bannerman." My companion was silenced, but I ventured a question. " How old is Spofforth ? " Pat came the answer, " Twenty-seven on the ninth of next month."

The crowd, including even the Parson, went

as quiet as a mouse as Barlow began the English bowling to Bannerman. Lyttelton, behind the wicket, crouched low. It was exactly a quarter past twelve. The next half-hour was a tumultuous prelude to the day. Bannerman was all vigilance, while Massie played one of the great innings of Test cricket. He hurled his bat at every ball the slightest loose, and his hits crashed ponderously to the boundary. He was the living image of defiance as he faced the Englishmen, glaring round the field his challenge. At one huge drive from Barlow's bowling my companion murmured, " I've never seen a bigger hit than that at the Oval." But the Parson overheard him. " When the Australians were here in '78," he said, " W. H. Game, playing for Surrey, hit a ball from Spofforth to square leg right out of the ground." Still, he admitted that this Massie fellow hit them quite hard enough. In half an hour England's advantage of 38 was gone. Hornby called up bowler after bowler, Studd for Barlow, Barnes for Studd. Steel tried his hand at 56—the sixth bowler in less than three-quarters of an hour. When Australia's score was 47 Massie lifted a ball to long on. " Lucas is there," said the Parson ; " he'll get it all r— Good Lord ! " For Lucas dropped the ball and blushed red as the crowd groaned out of its soul.

" Sixty-six for none," murmured the man at my side ; " they're 28 on with all their wickets intact. If Massie prevails—ah, bravo, sir ; well bowled, well bowled ! " A ball from Steel had tempted Massie, and just as he jumped out it broke back and wrecked the wicket. Massie walked to the pavilion, roared home by an admiring but much relieved crowd. His innings was worth 55 to Australia, made out of 66 in less than an hour.

Bonnor came next, and the English out-fields dropped deep and had apprehensive thoughts. Would not Massie's example make this bearded giant a very Jehu ? But Hornby has an inspiration. He asks Ulyett to bowl instead of Steel. And Ulyett moves to the wicket like a man ploughing against a breaker, puts the last ounce of his Yorkshire strength into a thunderbolt of a ball that sends Bonnor's middle stump flying. The crowd is only just getting back the breath lost in approval of this feat when Bannerman is caught by Studd at extra mid-off. Bannerman has batted seventy minutes for 13. " Quick work for him ! " says the Parson. And with the broad bat of Bannerman out of the way the English bowlers begin to see daylight. Peate's slow left-hand deliveries spin beautifully, as though controlled by a string. The Australians now, save Murdoch, are just guessing. The fourth wicket falls at 75, the fifth at 79. Australia are all out 122. " Only 85 to win," says the Parson. " It's our game after all, though Lucas did his best to lose it."

It was a true autumn afternoon going to its fall in grey light when " W. G." and Hornby went to the wicket to face Spofforth and Garratt. The crowd filled the ground, but so silent was it as Grace took his guard that one could hear the tink-tink of a hansom cab coming closer and closer along the Vauxhall Road. Spofforth's first over was fast—he let the ball go with a quick leap, dropping his arm at the moment of release. Blackham " stood back " when Grace was batting, but crept up for Hornby. " Beautiful wicket-keeping," murmured my companion. " Pinder was not less gifted," said the Parson. And he added, " I have not seen Spofforth bowl as fast as this for some time. He has latterly cultivated medium-pace variations." Both Hornby and Grace began confidently, and at once the tension lifted. Hornby made a lovely cut from Spofforth and a dainty leg stroke for a couple.

Spofforth uprooted Hornby's off stump with England's score 15, and with his next ball clean bowled Barlow. The crowd gave out a suspicion of a shiver, but the advent of bluff George Ulyett was reassuring, especially as Grace welcomed him with a fine leg hit from Garratt for three and a beautiful on drive to the boundary from Spofforth. " Thirty up," said my companion ; " only 55 to get." England was still 30 for two when Spofforth crossed over to the pavilion end. Now I was behind his arm ; I could see his superb breakback. And he bowled mainly medium pace this time. With each off break I could see his right hand, at the end of the swing over, finish near the left side, " cutting " under the ball. Sometimes his arm went straight over and continued straight down in the follow-through—and then the batsman had to tackle fierce top spin. There was the sense of the inimical in his aspect now. He seemed taller than he was a half-hour ago, the right arm of him more sinuous. There was no excitement in him ; he was, the Parson said, cold-blooded. Still Ulyett faced him bravely while Grace, at the other end, time after time moved from his crease with a solid left leg and

pushed the ball away usefully. " Fifty up,"
said my companion, " for two wickets. It's all
over—we want only 34 now." And at 51
Spofforth bowled a very fast one to Ulyett, who
barely snicked it. It served though ; Blackham
snapped the catch, and his " Hzat ! " was hoarse
and aggressive. Lucas came in, and with two
runs more " W. G." was caught at mid-off.
" What a stroke ! " said the Parson. " I'm afraid
he's not the Grace he was." Four for 53, and
Lyttelton and Lucas in. Lyttelton hits out big-
heartedly, but the field is like a net tightly drawn.
It is suddenly understood by every man of us that
the game is in the balance. " The wicket must
be bad," says somebody.

Lucas stonewalls, with a bat as straight as a
die. Spofforth bowls a maiden ; Boyle bowls a
maiden ; Spofforth bowls another maiden. The
air is growing thick. " Get runs or get out, for
the Lord's sake," says somebody. The field
creeps closer and closer to the wicket. Spofforth
and Boyle are like uncanny automatons, bowling,
bowling, bowling. . . . Six successive maidens.
" This," says the Parson, " this is intolerable."
One's heart is aching for an honest boundary hit.
. . . And the human bowling machines send
down six more successive maidens. Think of it ;
twelve successive maidens, and the game in that
state, the crowd in that purgatory. " When
Grace was a boy of eighteen I saw him make 50
on this very ground, and he played every ball he
got." It was the Parson again, but now he
sounded a little strained, a little unhappy. At
the end of the twelfth successive maiden, a hit
was purposely mis-fielded that Spofforth might

have a " go " at Lyttelton. The batsmen fell into the snare. Four more maidens, and spinning is Lyttelton's wicket. " Anyhow, that's over and done with ! " thankfully breathes the crowd. Better all be dead than dying ! England five for 66—19 needed. Steel comes next and Lucas hits a boundary. Roars the crowd " Bravo ! " then catches breath. Steel, caught and bowled Spofforth, none—Maurice Read clean bowled second ball. England seven for 70. " Incredible ! " say 20,000 people in dismal unison. Barnes, the next man, hits a two. Thirteen to win. Heaven bless us, Blackham has blundered ! He allows three byes. Run Barnes, run Lucas ! Spofforth is inscrutable as the crowd makes its noises. His next ball is too fast for eyes at the boundary's edge to see. Lucas comes down on it, though— hard, determined. And the ball rolls ever so gently on to the wicket and disturbs the bail. Poor Lucas bows his head and departs, and blasphemy is riot throughout the crowd and is communicated by stages to the outer darkness of Kennington Road. The stars are set against England—our cricketers are for the first time on English soil face to face with a victorious Aus- tralian XI. With ten to struggle for, Blackham catches Barnes off his glove, and the last man is here—poor Peate, who is the best slow bowler in England and not a bit more of a cricketer than that, and what good are his mysteries of spin now ? Studd is there yet, though ; only ten runs and it is our game. Perhaps *he*—Peate has hit a two. It was audacious, but maybe the ball was a safe one to tackle. A bad ball's a bad ball at any time. Peate has nerve (so we are telling ourselves, desperately) : he's the right man : he'll play the steady game to good stuff and leave the job to Studd. . . . The stark truth is that Peate hit out wildly yet again at a slow from Boyle, missed it, and was bowled. There was a hollow laugh somewhere as the wicket went back, but whether it came from this world or the next I couldn't say. Studd did not get a ball. " Why, man, did you try to hit : why couldn't you just stop them ? " they asked Peate. " Well," he replied, " I couldn't trust Maister Studd ! "

As Peate's wicket was broken, ten thousand people rushed the rails and hid the green field. Spofforth was carried shoulder - high to the pavilion, and there the mob praised a famous man. I, too, wanted to get up and shout, but somehow I was rooted to my seat. I was probably the only man in that multitude on the pavilion not standing up, and as I sat there I had a strange sense of making a lonely hole in a solid black mass. The Parson was standing on the seat beside me. His boots were not more than two feet from my eyes and I could see the fine ribbed work on the upper edge of the soles. The cheering came downwards to me, sounding remote. I lost grip on events. It seemed that I sat there till the ground was almost deserted, till over the field came a faint mist, and with it the vague melancholy of twilight in a great city. Time to go home, I thought . . . a great match . . . great days . . . great men . . . all gone . . . far away . . . departed glory. . . . A hand of some one touched my shoulder and I heard him say : " The Orsetralians are on the way, and they'll be in the nets at four o'clock. Nice in the sun, isn't it ? "

THE CHARM OF GOLF

A. A. Milne

WHEN he reads of the notable doings of famous golfers, the eighteen-handicap man has no envy in his heart. For by this time he has discovered the great secret of golf. Before he began to play he wondered wherein lay the fascination of it ; now he knows. Golf is so popular simply because it is the best game in the world at which to be bad.

Consider what it is to be bad at cricket. You have bought a new bat, perfect in balance ; a new pair of pads, white as driven snow ; gloves of the very latest design. Do they let you use them ? No. After one ball, in the negotiation of which neither your bat, nor your pads, nor your gloves come into play, they send you back into the pavilion to spend the rest of the afternoon listening to fatuous stories of some old gentleman who knew Fuller Pilch. And when your side takes the field, where are you ? Probably at long leg both ends, exposed to the public gaze as the worst fieldsman in London. How devastating are your emotions. Remorse, anger, mortification, fill your heart ; above all, envy—envy of the lucky immortals who disport themselves on the green level of Lord's.

Consider what it is to be bad at lawn tennis. True, you are allowed to hold on to your new racket all through the game, but how often are you allowed to employ it usefully ? How often does your partner cry " Mine ! " and bundle you out of the way ? Is there pleasure in playing football badly ? You may spend the full eighty minutes in your new boots, but your relations with the ball will be distant. They do not give you a ball to yourself at football.

But how different a game is golf. At golf it is the bad player who gets the most strokes. However good his opponent, the bad player has the right to play out each hole to the end ; he will get more than his share of the game. He need have no fears that his new driver will not be employed. He will have as many swings with it as the scratch man ; more, if he misses the ball altogether upon one or two tees. If he buys a new niblick he is certain to get fun out of it on the very first day.

And, above all, there is this to be said for golfing mediocrity—the bad player can make the strokes of the good player. The poor cricketer has perhaps never made fifty in his life ; as soon as he stands at the wickets he knows that he is not going to make fifty to-day. But the eighteen-handicap man has some time or other played every hole on the course to perfection. He has driven a ball 250 yards ; he has made superb approaches ; he has run down the long putt. Any of these things may suddenly happen to him again. And therefore it is not his fate to have to sit in the club smoking-room after his second round and listen to the wonderful deeds of others. He can join in too. He can say with perfect truth, " I once carried the ditch at the fourth with my second," or " I remember when I drove into the bunker guarding the eighth green," or even " I did a three at the eleventh this afternoon "—bogey being five. But if the bad cricketer says, " I remember when I took a century in forty minutes off Lockwood and Richardson," he is nothing but a liar.

For these and other reasons golf is the best game in the world for the bad player. And sometimes I am tempted to go further and say that it is a better game for the bad player than for the good player. The joy of driving a ball straight after a week of slicing, the joy of putting a mashie shot dead, the joy of even a moderate stroke with a brassie ; best of all, the joy of the perfect cleek shot—these things the good player will never know. Every stroke we bad players make we make in hope. It is never so bad but it might have been worse ; it is never so bad but we are confident of doing better next time. And if the next stroke is good, what happiness fills our soul. How eagerly we tell ourselves that in a little while all our strokes will be as good.

What does Vardon know of this ? If he does a five hole in four he blames himself that he did not do it in three ; if he does it in five he is miserable. He will never experience that happy surprise with which we hail our best strokes. Only his bad strokes surprise him, and then we may suppose that he is not happy. His length and accuracy are mechanical ; they are not the result, as so often in our case, of some suddenly applied maxim or some suddenly discovered innovation. The only thing which can vary in his game is his putting, and putting is not golf but croquet.

But of course we, too, are going to be as good as Vardon one day. We are only postponing the day because meanwhile it is so pleasant to be bad. And it is part of the charm of being bad at golf that in a moment, in a single night, we may become good. If the bad cricketer said to a good cricketer, " What am I doing wrong? " the only possible answer would be, " Nothing particular, except that you can't play cricket." But if you or I were to say to our scratch friend, " What am I doing wrong? " he would reply at once, " Moving the head " or " Dropping the right knee " or " Not getting the wrists in soon enough," and by to-morrow we should be different players. Upon such a little depends, or seems to the eighteen-handicap to depend, excellence in golf.

And so, perfectly happy in our present badness and perfectly confident of our future goodness, we long-handicap men remain. Perhaps it would be pleasanter to be a little more certain of getting the ball safely off the first tee ; perhaps at the fourteenth hole, where there is a right of way and the public encroach, we should like to feel that we have done with topping ; perhaps——

Well, perhaps we might get our handicap down to fifteen this summer. But no lower ; certainly no lower.

FAREWELL TO THE FAIR

Ivor Brown

On Easter Monday I walked on to Hampstead
Heath and took with me some boyhood memories
of the old and wanton festival with its big parade
of factory girls dancing to barrel organs in their
fine feathers and long yellow boots. In those
days there was lavish use of " the tickler," that
speedy weapon for the making of chance acquaintance. But now no eager merchants of the gutter
were massed in the heathward streets beseeching
us to " Tickle 'em up, sir. One penny, the
tickler." Nobody offered me a " Harry-Lauder-
Scottish-cap, one penny." Paper hats are now
as rare as that Edwardian flower the fancy waist-
coat ; they are not worn. In a prolonged evening
stroll I only bagged two lonely specimens of
jockey-cap, and the wearers looked self-con-
sciously defiant, as though they knew they had
done the wrong thing and were standing firm out
of bravado. As for men and women changing
hats—such Victorian gestures are museum antics
only.

The space given to the fair was smaller than
in pre-war times, and so was the crowd, a much
diminished and far more respectable assembly.
The only thing that seemed to have grown was

the mess. Bigger and beastlier litter is evidently a tacit slogan that attracts. People had taken special trouble to carry their papers to the neighbourhood of an official bin, and had then tossed them carefully all round the bin. Has all our anti-litter campaigning merely produced an angry opposition with a private system of forfeits for any member who puts his rubbish in the appointed receptacle ? In this squalor we retain our national taste for anarchy in entertainment. But the individual glories of the fair had vanished. The whole thing had become mechanized and, because mechanized, drab and joyless. There was a blare of tinned music but very little singing at night of the couples moving homeward. Above all, there was scarce a remnant of the good old rhetoric wherewith the sturdy magician or the pugilist would call attention to his booth. It was whoopee, I suppose, but whoopee without hosannas, a featureless revel that lacked its fine show of Bardolphian noses and of Pistolian braggadocio. Sobriety was rampant, and not in the alcoholic sense only.

I do not see how fairs can last much longer if they are going to be so uniform and so much of a pattern. In my Hampstead boyhood I paid my coppers to see rarer shows of all kinds : fat and boneless ladies, dwarfs, boxers, and a Giant Sewer Rat. I am not suggesting that such spectacles are an ideal entertainment for anybody ; but the fair had diversity and clamorous competition. There was always somebody roaring at you to step this way. And there were all sorts of wondrous fellows " doing their stuff " at the side of the Heath, men who broke stones with the naked hand, or swallowed swords, or were tied up in dozens of knots and then wriggled free, even though their bonds had been tied by the cunning hand of a sailor. There always used to be sailors in uniform at Hampstead on Bank Holiday ; one imagined them in tropic seas dreaming of this English felicity among the mud and flares and whelks with a spit of English rain in the cold wind. But this Easter Monday I saw no sailor, and I saw no costers and no ostrich plume.

Nothing is more irritating, and few things are more common, than a bogus sentimentality about caravans and circuses. A menagerie is a dismal and disgusting spectacle ; if anybody wants to see a mangy tiger pacing interminably round a tiny prison under the ceaseless provocation of the staring, tittering humans, or a school of performing dogs, he must have an extraordinary and a deplorable taste in fun. And if the whole human side of it stopped, nobody would be robbed of a decent or enviable way of living. To be a freak on view in a tent or to be the exploiter and promoter of a boxing booth into which a half-drunken navvy is lured with half a crown to have a smack at the kept negro bruiser, and to be smacked himself for the benefit of a twopenny audience— these are not occupations that deserve any encouragement in a civilized community. The caravan life may look fine and large in the faked gipsydom of films and fiction, but it must in fact be a cramped and dirty existence which compares poorly enough even with the ownership of a roof in the worst end of Mean Street. I recount, but I do not regret, the alteration of the personnel

who create an 'Appy 'Alf 'Oliday for Hampstead's
Festival visitors. If a man can do better for
himself by not breaking stones with the naked
hand and by not swallowing the more uncom-
fortable kinds of hardware, so much the better
for him. I cannot think that the old age of such
flesh-subduing mountebanks is usually " a sweet
serene." My point is that a fair, for good or
ill, depends on such primary qualities of appeal
as variety, simplicity, and individuality. All I
could discover at Hampstead was a showy spread
of swings and roundabouts, and a host of mechanical games of chance which our astounding
law, forbidding roulette, admits to be played for
the people's coppers. The people lose their
coppers rapidly and rather glumly. They lose
still more at the coconuts, which are now so
firmly fitted into their stands that it is almost
impossible to dislodge them. Why anybody
should want so repulsive an article as a coconut I
have no idea. But the notion has always existed
that the horrid thing is to be coveted, even at
much loss, and the losses are now larger, whereas
the coconuts are not. Another noticeable point
is the triumph of the mechanical swing-boat. In
the old kind of swing the height of your vessel's
transit was determined by your own energy, and
there would be hot rivalries of the will to altitude,
and furious competitions of gallantry and address.
But now you are attached to a seat in an " aerial
steam-boat " which pitches horribly, almost
achieving the full orbit of a circular course.
There is no skill or energy involved ; the test is
purely one of gastric endurance. That elimina-
tion of the individual energy is typical of the

up-to-date fair, in which nearly all the booths offer the same kind of attraction. They carry their own batteries and have electric illumination. They are more grandiose in aspect, and the prizes which you don't get have an air of being bigger and brighter. Possibly there are more of the mechanical contrivances which appear to have been designed as powerful emetics. But there is none of that showmanship which depends on lung-power, on the gift of the gab, and on that roaring immodesty which is the professional technique of the bookmaker and the auctioneer. If you are not having your stomach turned, or frittering away pence on some tedious game of chance, you have nothing to watch or listen to. There is none of the fun provided free for the urchin and at the cost of a coin in the hat for the more generous adults by all the streetside orators, pill-vendors, or masters of mystery. At last I found a fortune teller, complete with crystal bowl and offering to prophesy my career for threepence. For this sum he would also throw in a magic bean from Ancient Egypt, reputed to be the world's surest talisman and lucky charm. The run on old beans was so great that I could not wait to purchase at the prophet's shrine. But his success was informative. He did not trouble to shout and give us any finery of rhetoric about the black arts. There was no need. But at least he was dressed as an Egyptian ; he was grotesque, preposterous, and, above all, individual. If fairs are to flourish they must keep that spontaneity of the market-place ; they must be crude and colourful, and proud of just those qualities.

Perhaps the whole game is up. Hampstead's

visiting crowds are no longer crude and colourful ; no pearlies, no plumes, no yellow boots, no fancy vests, no East End girls in the purple. East Enders, perhaps, but art-silky, and dressed West-Endish, cinema-fed, charabanc carted, and, above all, sophisticated. I felt that they go to the fair with a second intention, patronizing it as a lark instead of accepting it as a splendid and simple catering for the holiday spirit. Meanwhile the fair itself becomes more and more mechanical, probably more remunerative to the owners of games of chance (witness the motor cars in which some of them arrived last Thursday, and which are now standing behind their pitches) but certainly less inventive. A fair ought to be wilder and odder and more human than the standardized sport of an Amusement Park. Have we said good-bye to all the elementary decorators of the plebeian carnival ? Have the black-faced banjo-men been silenced for ever by the grinding racket of amplified American tunes ? Even those Easter Monday regulars, the banner-bearers who announce that "The Wicked Shall be Turned to Hell," have disappeared. No doubt they have decided that fairing is no longer an ungodly occupation and has become too chilly a routine to lure the potential sons of Satan. They know best.

THE TRAGIC YEARS

E. M. Delafield

I⊤ is fatally easy to be sentimental over reminiscences of childhood. One is apt to see oneself as a wistful, pathetic, misunderstood little creature. And, indeed, to a certain extent, all children *are* wistful, pathetic, misunderstood little creatures. But they are also hard-hearted, egotistical, and uncivilized little creatures, and this aspect of childhood is all too seldom touched upon, even in fiction. In autobiography it is ignored altogether.

I propose, in fact, to ignore it myself.

No one who remembers me as a little girl has ever yet told me that I was a nice child. Occasionally, it has been said that I was an intelligent one, or a pretty one, or a precocious one. Far more often I have been assured that I was a spoilt child, a very tiresome child, and an exceedingly naughty child.

As a matter of fact, the consciousness of being a naughty child was early and thoroughly driven into me, and my consequent cast-iron conviction that I must eventually go to hell and burn there for ever and ever, would have done credit to any member of the Fairchild family. It overshadowed the whole of life for me, from the time I was

140

seven years old until long after I was, at least in the physical sense, " grown up."

Any reminiscences of my childhood, therefore, would make singularly gloomy reading—and the more honest they were, the gloomier they would be.

So that I propose to write freely of only one aspect of those days : that connected with the impulse that eventually led to my becoming a writer.

No one, so far as I know, has ever done me the disservice of preserving any of my early efforts in the field of literature ; but I have fairly vivid recollections of one or two unfinished master-pieces—usually in verse, and invariably tragic.

In those days, I liked an unhappy ending. I liked people to die, or to part from one another for ever, and I saw to it that in any composition of mine they did either one or the other, and very often both.

Indeed what strikes me most forcibly about my first attempts at writing, is the entire lack of humour that they evince, and the total absence of any feeling for reality. I had nearly added lack of originality as well ; but perhaps that is not quite fair, for although my point of view was purely imitative, I do remember occasional start-ling individualities of expression.

For instance, I solved the difficulty of finding a line to rhyme with my dying soldier's farewell to his love—" Good-bye for ever more, my darling "—as follows, " *I'm flying upward like a starling*," and this strange metaphor seemed to me not only ingenious, but highly poetical as well.

At seven or eight years old I began my first

novel, which was to be called *Sylvia's Lost Brother*, and opened with the disappearance, in a thick London fog, of the infant Edward—brother of the heroine. I wrote four chapters—I think they must have been very short ones—and the *dénouement* to come was clear in my mind.

Sylvia, years later, orphaned, and—I need hardly say—bereft of her lover, was to be living alone in London, when one night a burglar was to enter the house, to be subsequently revealed as the lost Edward, and to die at her feet.

It is melancholy to have to add that the black manuscript book containing the germ of this remarkable effort was thrown into the water-butt by a younger sister—the only wilful injury, I think, that she ever did me in her life—and never retrieved.

At eleven, in the intervals of writing quantities of sentimental and very, very tragic verse, I covered a great deal of paper with the story of the Hamiltons. That manuscript survived for some years, and I re-read it at a later and more critical age.

There were six Hamiltons, young and beautiful, and they had an unkind step-mother, and sooner or later they all died, excepting one called Marjory, who went to the bad in some unspecified way and lived in London ; but I feel sure that if I had ever finished the book she would have died too.

The Hamiltons, like King Charles, were an unconscionable time a-dying, and in the case of Eileen, aged twelve, the sentence " Her blue eyes opened for the last time " occurred sixteen times in five pages.

After I went to school I stopped writing, except

for a very occasional poem, until my sister and I started a private magazine. My contributions to it were numerous, and mostly very bad—all either pompous or sentimental. It was not until years later that it even occurred to me that one might possibly try, at least occasionally, to be amusing.

I was about fourteen when the story that was to be written and published long afterwards as *Zella Sees Herself*, first came into my mind. The character of Zella, the study of a very youthful *poseuse*, took shape almost exactly as I afterwards described her, but I meant the book to end—very characteristically—with Zella's suicide! When I eventually wrote it, however, I was in my twenties, and had at last outgrown my passion for tragedy.

The germ of *The Pelicans*—my third novel— also dates from my schoolroom days. I used to tell myself the story of the three girls, Rosamund, Frances, and Hazel, and of the boy, Morris, while I practised the piano. Neither the central characters, nor the story itself, underwent much alteration when I came to write the book, more than ten years later.

Like all imaginative children, I lived largely in a world peopled by characters of my own invention. Almost all of them, I think, eventually found their way into one or other of my books. The excessive virtue and beauty of the women, and the tendency towards unbridled heroism and self-sacrifice of the men, had to be brought into line with the prosaic laws that govern life as it really is, but their fundamental characteristics, on the whole, remained unaltered.

What did alter, fortunately for me, was the profound and humourless gloom of my own outlook on life. But long before that amendment had taken place, the difficult, bewildering, often despairing, days of childhood were over.

THE MATRIX OF LONDON

James Bone

LONDON goes to Portland for its stone much as Rome goes to Carrara for its marble. It has been so since Wren journeyed to the little Dorsetshire peninsula—still called an isle, though connected by a gravel isthmus to the mainland—to choose his stone for St. Paul's, marking some sample blocks with his " Y " that can still be seen there. It was so one day last week when Mr. Charles Holden, the architect of the new London University buildings, came down with Dr. Deller, the Principal of the University, and a small party to select some of the stone for those buildings which, when carried to their completion—perhaps thirty years from now—will require more stone than St. Paul's itself.

It is strange to think of these masses of limestone that have lain through uncounted ages in the Dorsetshire ground being seized and taken to London and fashioned into its chief glories. The stone, the accretion of sea creatures, goes to fashion our most gigantic buildings, and they can be discerned in them, for, despite all the care of masons and builders, cockle shells, oyster shells, and sea-urchins will be found in the walls and towers of the best Whitbed stone. You can feel the oyster edges in the plinth of King Charles's monument at Charing Cross, and see the shell called " horses' heads " in the parapet of Bush House. St. Paul's, even to its stone prophets on the roof, is stamped with the secret seal of these marine creatures, as though Britannia herself had put them there. But architect, builder, and mason like them not, for the fewer the shells the better the stone. Despite Mr. E. E. Way, the head of the Barnes Company, who are delivering the stone, despite Mr. Pollinger, the most expert of head masons—despite every one, the sea creatures will somehow register that it is their stone.

It was on a windy, showery day that we drove along the Chesil Beach, a narrow neck of pebbles forming a ridge just wide enough to bear a railway and a road to the isle, and climbed four hundred feet on the zig-zag road to its tableland, where lie the quarries from which so much of London arose, and in which so much of the London of the future waits. One could not but feel that another chapter in its long history was being written as the little group of people in waterproofs picked their way from quarry to quarry, and Mr. Holden scrutinized the stone—hewn in great, untrimmed shape or in its bed in the quarry—that is to rise in ordered masses and tower to be a landmark of learning in London through centuries to come. All England's notable architects had come here for their stone, most of them in person : Inigo Jones for his banqueting-hall in Whitehall, and Wren for his cathedral and all his churches. To have the opportunity to design a building in Portland stone is still the dream of the young architect, even in these shabby, concrete days. We were visiting the matrix of London's grandeur.

Your first surprise is the size of the famous isle—the " Isle of Slingers," as the Romans called it—which is only four miles long and a mile and a half wide. The second is that the quarrymen who provide the stone number less than six hundred, and the masons who trim and dress the stone only some three hundred and fifty, so, including the labourers who work about the quarries, the whole industry is probably only a thousand strong, although surely no battalion in the world has produced so magnificent and lasting an output.

The Portland folk even to-day are a community with racial and social characteristics of their own, not much changed since Hardy wrote of them in *The Pursuit of the Well Beloved*. By ancient right they alone can work in the quarries, and if a Portland lass marries a " Kimberlin " (a foreigner from the mainland), he does not legally acquire that right, but their son does. Many " Kimberlins " are permitted to work in the mason's sheds. The natives still own a good deal of the quarry land and lease it to the quarrying companies who run the stone industry.

Portland men never go to other quarries. The tractable and accommodating nature of the stone needs a particular kind of working different from quarrying other stone. The land is scored with fissures running north and south, with some breaks running east and west, so that open quarrying can go on with advantages unknown elsewhere. Once the top part is blasted or cut away, the stone can be split by wedges and "feathers" through the Whitbed, which is usually in three layers of about five feet deep, separated by "bars" of inferior stone. The men work in gangs of eight, with steam or electric crane, or four with hand hoist. Often each gang is a family. One elderly giant, with a vast waistline and thickets of eyebrow, we saw working with his seven lithe sons like the hero of a saga. The men, as a whole, are remarkably handsome, with Mediterranean brown face and arms, wielding their heavy axes with grace in their skill. The young men favour white cotton shirts and white berets.

Small as the island is, the quarries do not intrude on your notice. We turned here and there from the roads and, following a break in the land, found ourselves in earshot of a continual pecking and tapping noise, and saw in a deep fissure with Cyclopean masses of cut stone piled at one side and shoals of stone debris and, on the other, the naked face of the rock ending in a deep cleft below us. Other quarries were semicircular, with the men working at the bottom. An enormous amount of waste stone has to be quarried and disposed somewhere to allow the Whitbed stone to be worked—almost half of the labour of the men goes to that unprofitable job. In one place we saw a vast accumulation of rubble placed on a field thirty years ago now being removed again as the quarry reached the field. The ordinary section of a good quarry shows rubble 30 feet, cap 11 feet, skull-cap 4 feet, roach 4 to 8 feet, Whitbed 15 to 17 feet in three tiers. The "bars," harder and shellier, between these tiers are now being split and polished and used for the panelling and lining of buildings. Roach, being very hard, rough, and expensive to work, is little used for buildings. The Whitbed, of course, is the cream of the stone—smooth and clean without discolorations, easy to work, and capable of enduring the London acids beyond other stones. In London it turns the familiar silvery hue, with deep black and purples where the rains do not wash it clean, so that, with the rain-bearing south-west wind in his mind, a sailor might find his direction through London by observing the weathering on its tall buildings and columns—whitest at the south-west, darkest at the north-east. The drip from cornices and mouldings also helps these discolorations. The romantic mystery of the face of London in this contradiction made by the black-and-white weathering of her Portland stone, with the appearance of shadows where there are no shadows and darkness where you expect light.

The architect and his party visited several quarries. At Rufus Castle we gazed along the shore at the mass of boulders and debris and cut stone at the undercliff that is called " The Weirs." Here the contractors of Wren cut the stone for St. Paul's from the edge of the plateau and shipped it off in ketches to London from a little quay that can still be seen. The Wren quarry is still called St. Paul's, but the natives call it by the old name of " Shepherd's Dinner." The Wakeham quarry, where some of the stone is being cut for London University, is not far away and on the same strata of the stone.

From Wakeham was taken the stone of the new Midland Bank in Manchester, which is using altogether four thousand tons. Mr. Vincent Harris's Manchester Library comes from another quarry in that neighbourhood, so that the stone of these two buildings lay in the Dorsetshire ground at much the same distance from each other as the buildings stand from one another in Manchester. Part of the Ship Canal building also came from Wakeham. At Weston quarry we saw the hole whence the modern front of Buckingham Palace came, and as we moved about the island we were told " the Royal Exchange of London was taken out of that bit "; " the Royal Automobile Club came out of the back of that quarry." But you cannot see the little quarry across the street from Avice Caro's cottage whence the Cenotaph was taken, for that is now earthed over again, with a garden on the top.

ROME

Norman Douglas

THE railway station at Rome has put on a new face. Blown to the winds is that old dignity and sense of leisure. Bustle everywhere ; soldiers in line, officers strutting about ; feverish scurryings for tickets. A young baggage employé, who allowed me to effect a change of raiment in the inner recesses of his department, alone seemed to keep up the traditions of former days. He was unruffled and polite ; he told me, incidentally, that he came from ——. That was odd, I said ; I had often met persons born at ——, and never yet encountered one who was not civil beyond the common measure. His native place must be worthy of a visit.

" It is," he replied. " There are also certain fountains . . ."

That restaurant, for example—one of those few for which a man in olden days of peace would desert his own tavern in the town—how changed ! The fare has deteriorated beyond recognition. Where are those succulent joints and ragoûts, the aromatic wine, the snow-white macaroni, the café-au-lait with genuine butter and genuine honey ?

War-time !

Conversed awhile with an Englishman at my side, who was gleefully devouring lumps of a particular something which I would not have liked to touch with tongs.

" I don't care what I eat," he remarked.

So it seemed.

I don't care what I eat : what a confession to make ! Is it not the same as saying, I don't care whether I am dirty or clean ? When others tell me this, I regard it as a pose, or a poor joke. This person was manifestly sincere in his profession of faith. He did not care what he ate. He looked it. Were I afflicted with this peculiar ailment, this attenuated form of *coprophagia*, I should try to keep the hideous secret to myself. It is nothing to boast of. A man owes something to those traditions of our race which has helped to raise us above the level of the brute. Good taste in viands has been painfully acquired ; it is a sacred trust. Beware of gross feeders. They are a menace to their fellow-creatures. Will they not act, on occasion, even as they feed ? Assuredly they will. Everybody acts as he feeds.

Then lingered on the departure platform, comparing its tone with that of similar places in England. A mournful little crowd is collected here. Conscripts, untidy-looking fellows, are leaving—perhaps for ever. They climb into those tightly packed carriages, loaded down with parcels and endless recommendations. Some of the groups are cheerful over their farewells, though the English note of deliberate jocularity is absent. The older people are resigned ; in the features of the middle generation, the parents, you may read a certain grimness and hostility to fate ; they are the potential mourners. The weeping note predominates among the sisters and children, who give themselves away pretty freely. An infectious thing, this shedding of tears. One little girl, loth to part from that big brother, contrived by her wailing to break down the reserve of the entire family. . . .

It rains persistently in soft, warm showers. Rome is mirthless.

There arises, before my mind's eye, the vision of a sweet old lady friend who said to me, in years gone by :

" When next you go to Rome, please let me know if it is still raining there."

It was here that she celebrated her honeymoon —an event which must have taken place in the 'sixties or thereabouts. She is dead now. So is her husband, the prince of moralizers, the man who first taught me how contemptible the human race may become. Doubtless he expired with some edifying platitude on his lips and is *deblatterating* them at this very moment in Heaven, where the folks may well be seasoned to that kind of talk.

Let us be charitable, now that he is gone !

To have lived so long with a person of this incurable respectability would have soured any ordinary woman's temper. Hers it refined ; it made her into something akin to an angel. He was her cross ; she bore him meekly and not, I like to think, without extracting a kind of sly, dry fun out of the horrible creature. A past master in the art of gentle domestic nagging, he

153

made everybody miserable as long as he lived, and I would give something for an official assurance that he is now miserable himself. He was a worm ; a good man in the worse sense of the word. It was the contrast—the contrast between his gentle clothing and ungentle heart, which moved my spleen. What a self-sufficient and inhuman brood were the Victorians of that type, hag-ridden by their nightmare of duty ; a brood that has never yet been called by its proper name. Victorians ? Why, not altogether. The mischief has its roots farther back. Addison, for example, is a fair specimen.

Why say unkind things about a dead man ? He cannot answer back.

Upon my word, I am rather glad to think he cannot. The last thing I ever wish to hear again is that voice of his. And what a face : gorgonizing in its assumption of virtue ! Now the whole species is dying out, and none too soon. Graft abstract principles of conduct upon natures devoid of sympathy and you produce a monster ; a sanctimonious fish ; the coldest beast that ever infested the earth. This man's affinities were with Robespierre and Torquemada — both of them actuated by the purest intentions and without a grain of self-interest : pillars of integrity. What floods of tears would have been spared to mankind had they only been a little corrupt ! How corrupt a person of principles ? He lacks the vulgar yet divine gift of imagination.

That is what these Victorians lacked. They would never have subscribed to this palpable truth : that justice is too good for some men, and not good enough for the rest. They cultivated the Cato or Brutus tone ; they strove to be stern old Romans—Romans of the sour and imperfect Republic ; for the Empire, that golden blossom, was to them a period of luxury and debauch. Nero—most reprehensible ! It was not Nero, however, but our complacent British reptiles, who filled the prisons with the wailing of young children, and hanged a boy of thirteen for stealing a spoon. I wish I had it here, that book which everybody ought to read, that book by George Ives on the History of Penal Methods— it would help me to say a few more polite things. The villainies of the virtuous : who shall recount them ? I can picture this vastly offensive old man acting as judge on that occasion and then, his " duties towards society " accomplished, being driven home in his brougham to thank Providence for one of those succulent luncheons, the enjoyment of which he invariably managed to ruin for every one except himself.

God rest his soul, the unspeakable phenomenon ! He ought to have throttled himself at his mother's breast. Only a woman imbued with ultra- terrestrial notions of humour could have tolerated such an infliction. Anybody else would have poisoned him in the name of Christian charity and common sense, and earned the gratitude of generations yet unborn.

Well, well ! R.I.P. . . .

SECRECY AND EVELINA

Sylva Norman

EVERY goose girl imagines herself, at some time, a princess. If she did not, she would be less than the very geese (which have, after all, a downy whiteness much to be admired against green grass). The born princess, if rarer, is as commonplace. She is too conversant with the details of gold plate and jewels and brocaded gowns, walks always stiffly on an over-polished floor, and meets deference with a yawn behind her fan. There is no breeze, romance, or laughter. Lacking the boldness to believe herself a goose girl, the princess is uninterested and bored.

Not one in millions has the best of both lives, being simultaneously a genuine goose girl and a real princess. That delicious, rollicking duality, like all ideal states, is seldom reached, and then soon fades away. But while it lasts it is a glorious game. It runs like this : every one knows you for a goose girl, and every one is intrigued by a particular princess. They prattle to you of the latter with ridiculous deference, while treating you with innocence or scorn. So you take the skin off human foibles, and examine them at your impish, hidden ease. A game for sly rogues only. We should all be glad to play it. The difficulties are, first, to be a downright, a notorious goose girl, and, secondly, to achieve your secret rank.

There are two exquisite examples, if no more. The first, so universal that she has no date, was nicknamed Cinderella. The second, whose name was really Frances, was known better as Fanny, even Fannikin. Over a century and a half ago she played her game. It was 1778 that saw (but blindfold) " the first publication of the ingenious, learned, and most profound Fanny Burney." That was to her diary, privately. To the world it would seem different. Short of Cinderella and her household chores, a better goose girl never was displayed. A child so shy and backward that at eight years old she does not know her letters, and is called by all her mother's friends " the little dunce." You may see her, the poor blockhead, wrinkling her forehead in all innocence over a book presented to her upside down. Two years later she is no less foolish. Having learnt to write now, she insists on scribbling nonsense on her own account, instead of profiting, as a grave and serious-minded creature would, by the educative words from other pens. " Fancy the Cinder-slut at a ball ! " wise souls protest. " How the whole Court would laugh ! "

Absurd, of course. So Cinderella goes back to the fireplace, and Fanny, with mixed shame and resolution, makes a bonfire of her scraps and scribblings, ruthlessly. But it is all no use. The princess motive haunts them still, and will not be banished. Till one night Cinderella picks a pumpkin in the moonlit garden, goes through sundry other rites, and stands transformed. As for the little dunce, that immolation on the paved court out of doors has had its consequences. Caroline Evelyn, it is true, was burnt with all solemnity, but her infant daughter was preserved and sheltered in a nook of Fanny's mind, and there she grew to unconfessed maturity, appearing later—like the children fairies steal—as a charming orphan in her native land.

An unknown lady danced all evening with the prince—and even Mr. Lowndes, the publisher, was kept in ignorance of his author's name. One Grafton, at the Orange Coffee House, was all he knew. Then the real sport began. The beautiful stranger was admired by every one; and " Evelina " made a genuine stir. Friends, acquaintances, discussed and commented. They made wild guesses at identity. But Cinderella! But Fanny! *They* never came into it—they were known. The goose girl always is known; better than she knows herself. Her outlines are immutable and rigid. She could never be the jewelled stranger, nor the author of a brilliant work. She is just Cinders who scrubs floors, or Fanny who grew up to destroy her idle scribblings and take to needlework. Of course, there are sundry people in the secret—a godmother, a lexicographer, and the like. They serve to whet the public interest by constant reference to the subject, until, to the unsuspected, gloating heroine, it appears to fill the world.

How Fanny revelled in her secret crowing! With what gusto she recorded all the comments— because, to be sure, they were all favourable, and, seeing the situation from all sides, she could sharpen it confidently into full significance by a bright egotistic comment of her own. " How much in luck," she exclaims of one admirer, " would she have thought herself had she known *who* heard her ! " Conceited ? But so naïvely, so exultantly, and with such awareness of the princess-goose girl in her character, that you cannot help loving it and sharing in the sport. Her diary is one burst of twinkling excitement over " Evelina " and the sly deception. For this one year life means only that. There is never any need to doubt its value. Had not it been vouched for by no less than Dr. Johnson ? Richardson, he had it, would have been afraid of Fanny—Harry Fielding too. Those inclined to scoff at " Evelina " changed their tone on hearing how the Doctor had been caught in admiration, when Mrs. Thrale deposited a volume as travelling companion in his coach.

Yes, she was no imaginary princess ; and yet the true delight, that touched the very tingling nerves of joy, was in the secrecy. " Nothing can be more ridiculous than the scenes in which I am perpetually engaged." " How many ridiculous things have I heard upon this subject ! " The word " ridiculous " was never employed more lovingly, and with more appreciation. Those " ridiculous things " are all down in the diary, together with Fanny's impish answers, subter- fuges, blushes. You would hardly believe she had laboured on a novel. She seemed a child presented with this moonlike toy of bright success and dear concealment. No triumph was too small to be recalled :

" ' A'n't you sorry this sweet book is done ? '
said Mrs. Gast.

" A silly little laugh was the answer.

" ' Ah ! ' said Patty, ' 'tis the sweetest book !
Don't you think so, Miss Burney ? '

" *N.B.*—Answer as above.

" ' Pray, Miss Fan,' says Mrs. Hamilton, ' who
wrote it ? '

" ' Really I never heard.'

" ' Cute enough that, Miss Sukey ! ' "

There is the goose girl with her " silly little
laugh " ! You can almost hear her pride in
even that. Just as Cinderella listened open-
mouthed and with her stupidest expression to
her sisters' praises of the fair unknown.

There are dramatic moments also—when the
princess-goose girl takes to flight. Cinderella
fled, in fear lest they should see her as a goose
girl ; Fanny, strangely, lest she be revealed as
a princess. During conversation about " Evelina,"
Fanny, when her wit and calmness failed her,
was for ever taking headers from the room. On
one occasion she was half-choked by a biscuit,
and obliged to call for water to wash it down.
" I was so much agitated by the certainty of
being known as a scribbler, that I was really ill
all night, and could not sleep." It sounds to us
delightfully affected ; but we must first subtract
the century and a half. If her confession is not
utterly sincere, yet it has a teaspoonful of truth
in it. We can guess at another cause for agita-
tion : she should have acknowledged—as she did
when it was over—that regret for her fading, sly
duality had first place. But in the second was

this trouble of the "scribbler." Here is what
dates Fanny as eighteenth century, and supplies
a reason (less intimate and naughty than the
real one) for her tenacious stealth. Inverted as
it seems, yet in this matter of female authorship it was deemed all right to be a goose
girl; the princess, on the contrary, was held
in shame.

Fanny need not have been worried. By her
very trickery she heard frank opinions, and
although the earlier burden was " He must be a
man of great abilities," the sex soon altered, and
without any accompanying contempt. Who could
afford to scorn an authoress whose book was
praised by Johnson, and had kept Burke glued
to it all night ? No, Miss Burney ; you were
not entitled, on that plea, to choke over a biscuit
or to lie awake. You saw the goose girl dying—
that was why the biscuit stuck so cruelly in your
throat.

For the glass slipper had to find its home eventually. There was a final frolic when Sir Joshua
Reynolds's nieces tried it first on Mrs. Thrale.
That impish lady thrust her foot out, and it
seemed to fit. She might have worn it, too,
indefinitely; but, instead, she flourished it for
an hour or so, and permitted its transference to
the rightful foot. Fanny was seen then in her
dignity as a real princess ; receiving awestruck
homage, gazing with the tragic eyes of desperation
after her dead dualism, her precious lost concealment in the goose girl's shell :

" Here, therefore, end all my hopes of secrecy !
I take leave of them with the utmost regret, and

though never yet was any scribbler drawn more honourably, more creditably, more partially into notice, I nevertheless cannot persuade myself to rejoice in the loss of my dear old obscurity."

There was the rub. She had the name, she had the fame, but she was forced to end the game. Henceforward Fanny is a little older. She must bear her own responsibilities of authorship; her behaviour must be that of the princess. She is no longer just " our Fanny," but a novelist— approached and scanned and criticized as a celebrity must be. "Well," she overhears, "you do not find Miss Burney quite so tremendous a person as you expected?" There is no call to gloat in secret over *that*. The advantage now is all against her—she is out on show. She has only to fear now for her next production, lest it should not reach the standard of the first.

Fame is, in fact, a deadly serious matter, now there are no secrets. It is either in jeopardy or coldly drab. But let no one sympathize with Fanny's sadness. She had months and months of playful, sheer exuberance, concrete and defined. For most of us, the best in this kind are but shadows, and even so, imagination is at work on them. How magnificent, how impossible, through our shower of labelled literature, to be a princess-goose girl! In what gathering, to begin with, would you find one book discussed so long and so exclusively, unless it had enraged a Home Secretary or Scotland Yard? When there are a thousand Cinderellas, the prince can barely spare a dance for each, nor will identity haunt him overmuch. It is a pity. Mr. Grafton at the Orange Coffee House will have the laugh on us if we attempt it. We must be content to watch that elf in Fleet Street, looking discreetly out at the shop door lest Mr. Lowndes should see her grin at him.

STUDENT DAYS

Storm Jameson

THOSE were queer, lively years. We felt, as every
one who was young with us felt, that we were
beginning a new age. So we were, but we were
misinformed on a vital detail. The arts, we
thought, were stirring in their sleep. Even the
novel—you can't conceive the effect on us of
The New Machiavelli. It scarcely seems possible
now that we took that so hard. But think that
to us the rigid Victorian code was still real. It
was something we had consciously to reject. We
saw it as narrow, timid, and cruel, and not at all
as a hard self-discipline or as an ideal. We were
not easy about it. We talked of our freedom
from this, that, and the other, but in our minds
the Victorian habit persisted, like an old coat
hung behind the door, that we shall one day take
down and put on. In the meantime we talked,
and ran about London looking for second-hand
copies of Anatole France, or stood in the rain to
listen to Socialist speeches, indifferent, because
we had heard it before, and yet believing in it and
in fraternity and equality and all that.

It is very hard to recall days when everything
was new and of interest. We were all then
absurdly hopeful, tireless, and confident. In

those days it would not have crossed my mind that I might fail or be hurt to death.

I cannot remember which year, whether spring or autumn, we saw the post-impressionist paintings. We had never seen any until this. Sydney and I went, expecting to laugh, and came away filled with an amazing excitement. We were so stirred that we walked about in the rain, half shouting. And now I cannot even remember the pictures, except for a Cézanne that remains in my mind because of one most lovely sunlit wall. I would give anything to feel again that supreme exhilaration. We went again a day or two later, taking O. Harland with us. Out of perversity (as I feel sure) he said he loathed the new painting. He said it was indecent, like a tipsy old woman kicking up her heels. We dragged him out, hot and vexed. He halted us in front of a policeman in the doorway, and asked him what he thought of the pictures.

" Nothing very much," the policeman said.

" There you are," he shouted at us. " It's your over-sophisticated minds that make you admire that muck. The pure, untutored mind of democracy can see what a sham it all is."

Still shouting furiously at each other, we went to a Lipton's café and ate a quantity of black sticky cake, such as only pure untutored stomachs can digest. Afterwards we went to a Wagner concert and quarrelled all the way home—I detested Wagner in those days. There was a thick fog. We climbed on to the bus at Waterloo Station and took the front seats outside. Sydney leaned out over the front. " Driver! drive like hell to Camberwell Green," he said. The man drove straight into a lamp-post. There was a great noise of broken glass and some shouts and then the driver's angry voice putting the entire blame for the accident on us. Most unfairly, I think.

Sometimes we went to a music hall—I feel very sorry for the young who never heard Marie Lloyd—she was herself " infinite variety," and the entire programme of the new non-stop shows is a thinner entertainment. She could make you laugh until you cried, but one or two of her songs were so harsh that the tears came first. The very way she glanced at you, with that mingling of hard cynical mirth, boldness, and an indescribable air of having been *used*, was like being slapped in the face by life. Have you ever lived in Brixton ? We walked about it several times a week, and it always made me think of Marie Lloyd—there was one big glaring shop in which, for all the lavishness of display, you never forgot that money has to be earned ; in a street under the railway, open stalls of butchers' meat, artificial silk stockings, oranges, the market of the slums ; streets of sordid houses ; streets of tall, once-genteel houses on the defensive behind spoiled gardens ; the respectability of Tulse Hill and the squalor of Kennington : the whole of it rank with life, life oozing between the bricks, strong, ugly, bitter, nasty, beautiful, and unabateable. That was Marie Lloyd. She's dead now—and I daresay Brixton is different. And one day they'll clean it up. It will be a good riddance—but it's queer to think that whatever else a safe, clean, orderly world produces it won't be able to produce a Marie Lloyd.

One of her favourite eating-places was in Brixton. It was called Biucchi's, and I think it was in a basement. I remember that once at eleven o'clock at night O. Harland and I were coming home through Brixton. I was tired and lagged, and he was losing patience with me. Suddenly he stood still, the light from a street lamp falling on him in blue-white splinters and wedges. "Where did you lunch?" he said. I couldn't remember. At last I said I thought I must have forgotten to eat any lunch. "You didn't have any dinner. Did you get your tea?" Surprised, I understood now why I was so tired. "You are a calf," he said angrily: "how much money have you got?" We turned out both our pockets, and made between us three and six. Would you believe it, Biucchi's was able to serve hot chicken at eleven at night? That was for me—O. Harland had coffee only, and watched me eat.

Another place was in Richmond. Nearly at the top of the hill there was a charming house in which the rooms were furnished with deep pile carpets, gate-legged tables, and deep, soft arm-chairs. Teas were a shilling a head, and they used to place uncut cakes on the table and leave you to help yourself. Of course the idea was that the lovers for whom the elegant rooms were meant would be feeling too delicate to eat.

But the best was Appenrodt's Lager Hall, in Coventry Street. I suppose we went there a dozen times in all—when one of us had just been sent money. You went downstairs, and there was the wide room, with the German inscriptions on the walls, and the quick friendly waiters, and now and then a deep blurred voice speaking German. The smells of cigar smoke and coffee blended in the warm air. I remember a very large German woman, fair, with brown sleepy eyes. She spread her arms, letting her furs slip to the floor, and said, " So will ich sie selbst essen." The way she spoke, rolling her eyes, and the foreign words, made it seem rich and mysterious, and made us look at each other and half feel that we had been caught into a strange town. I watched, fascinated, her thick white fingers stripping the skin from the fruit.

There was something very good, friendly, and stolid about that place. Everything was good— the food, the coffee, the waiters—and yet if you were shabby it did not matter. You could still sit there and take your ease. It is one of the things that were lost to London during the war. It has never been replaced—perhaps it is irreplaceable, but upon my soul I do grudge it. So I do the Viennese café that used to stand at the corner of Hart Street and New Oxford Street. Once I had coffee and brioches there in the middle of the morning—I now forget who took me there and paid for it. But the Viennese brioches were delicious, and I made myself a promise that when I could afford it I would come here often for breakfast. Alas, that long narrow room is now a bank. Could any war-change be more sordid or more typical of a spoiled London ?

There cannot have been four shabbier poor scholars in London. But neither had any poor scholar a life so finely gay. We were not taxpayers or citizens, we had no business to call us to regular lives, we ate meals that other people had prepared, and took no thought for the morrow, how we should eat, or wherewithal we should be clothed. Like that we were happy, because we were outside the machine. As soon as that vagabond life comes to an end, when from poor scholars you become tax-payers, heads of families, and what not, you may be comfortable, but are you happy? Of course not. You have possessions—and that alone is enough to destroy your peace of mind. Besides, you have become conscious of time. You feel its works in your bones, like the death-watch beetle in an ageing fabric. You have responsibilities, you reckon up your income, buy books, houses, pictures, beds, tables, electric sweepers, run a business, write books, travel, get children, tune-in to Daventry for the news, vote, save money, buy a piece of land for a grave. I have been happier than any woman. But in those days I was happy and (to cram up into a word what is too complex to be said in a page) free.

Towards Christmas we bought a flagon of Australian burgundy. It was vile stuff. We drank it late at night round the fire, and ate toasted muffins and sardines. This is true, and I live.

WITCHES AND WHATNOT

E. V. Knox

THERE is a recent tendency in English literature which I find a little peculiar. It is not so much a frank, open-minded tolerance of witchcraft, voodooism, magical rites, incantations, and heathen sacrifice such as might be expected from persons of intellect and culture. It is more than that. It is a desire to plunge into these things and wallow in their midst ; to take part in the rites of oboi and gaga, to collect herbs under the moonlight and make soup with them, to practise in very truth the mysteries of the old Incas of Peru and the old Iguanas of Honduras ; to make one's way into the most difficult jungles of Central Africa or Central America, tattoo oneself all over, put a ring through one's nose, and, if possible, to lap blood.

There is a distinct change here between our present attitude and that of Victorian literature. Victorian literature, on the whole, was inclined to censure the heathen in his blindness for bowing down to wood and stone. Or, if not, it took the even colder attitude of censuring people for bowing down to any kind of deity whatever. An earnest advocacy of demoniac dances, a bigoted belief in witch-doctors breathes through the pages of none of the great poets or novelists of those bygone days. But now it is quite otherwise.

At any moment, I gather, a young girl may start up and say to her mother, " I am tired of this feverish and outworn civilization. I am going out and away to the far places of Mexico to find a strong, vivid, brown-limbed people who practise the old faith of the Mayas. I mean to wander amongst them until they take me away into the mountain fastnesses and drug me with strange herbs, and then at last lead me to the sacrificial chamber. And there, at the moment when the shaft of the sun strikes the altar, they will lay me on the cold stone and sacrifice me, and I shall know a completeness and a contentedness beyond imagination, and beyond dream."

" Yes, dear," says her mother ; " when do you want to start ? "

" This very afternoon."

" I wish you could put it off till to-morrow, dear, because the Smiths are coming to-night, and I hoped you would arrange the flowers for dinner."

But the young girl is obdurate, and goes to look up the rail and steamer services to Popocatepetl at once.

Just as she starts, her mother, moist-eyed, presses into her hands a hot-water bottle with a knitted cover, for she cannot help feeling how cold it will be out there on the sacrificial stone amongst the Maya priests and priestesses.

" Of course I know the child must arrange her own life," she murmurs to herself as the taxicab departs for Waterloo.

Or another young girl will say quite suddenly at breakfast :

" By the way, Dad, I have decided to become a witch."

" Oh, yes," says her father, frowning a little over the top of the *Times*. " When do you want to begin ? "

" Almost at once. I thought of getting a few toads together to-day and buying some simples and a one-eyed cat. I've seen a heavenly little cottage down in Hertfordshire that would be just the thing, and I want you to buy it for me, please."

" You won't make much of a living out of it, will you ? " he grumbles, as he adjusts his spectacles and writes out the cheque.

" Oh, but of course I shall, Dad. I shall make little wax images to stick through with pins for people who want to put evil spells on their neighbours, and I shall brew hell-broths and love-philtres, and cure people's rheumatism by making ointment from mouse-fat for them. I can have no end of a good time."

" Very well, then," he growls. " Wilkins will take you down in the Daimler."

And off she goes too.

And now, last of all, I find the book of a man who has penetrated to the very centre of Haiti, and shared with really simple faith and enthusiasm in the fine old secret orgies of Voodoo, which those of our ancestors who knew anything about them always thought were things to be discouraged as compared with muscular Christianity and cold morning baths.

The author is a Mr. W. B. Seabrook, who, it appears, has done very good work previously in Arabia amongst the Bedouins and Druses, and whirling dervishes and devil-worshippers. But he has done better, I should say, in Haiti. He saw some really jolly religious ceremonies out there.

"In the actual slaying of the sacrificial beasts which now began, accompanied by deep chanting, there was no savagery, no needless cruelty, no lust of killing. It was a solemn ritual business, though, when once it began, it moved swiftly. A goat was held by the horns, the sharp-edged *machete* drawn across the throat by a *papeloi*, and the blood gushed into a wooden bowl. . . . And the bull, before whom, deified, the blood of these other beasts had been poured out as an offering, must also die. . . . The blood did not gush fountain-like, as it had from the cut throats of the goats ; it spurted in a hard, small stream from the bull's pierced side. . . . The *papeloi* and *mameloi* now both drank ceremonially of the holy blood, and then, amid the crescendo excitement and surging forward of the worshippers, the twenty women robed in white danced in a group, leaping and whirling like frenzied maenads. . . . It was savage and abandoned, but it seemed to me magnificent and not devoid of a certain beauty. Something inside myself awoke and responded to it."

It would. That is always the way it happens in these modern books. Something very deep and innate, and primitive and holy stirs in the heart of the watcher as soon as the knife-slashing and yelling and eyeball rolling begin, and they feel that all is right in the best of possible worlds.

After that Mr. Seabrook saw another ceremony, where the spirit of a girl passed magically into

" a sturdy brown young goat with big blue, terrified, almost human eyes," and then the goat was killed and its blood passed round.

" So the bowl itself was held to my lips, and three times I drank. The blood had a clean, warm, salty taste."

That causes me no particular surprise. Any one who has had a tooth knocked out will have discovered this without having gone to Haiti. But the point is that Mr. Seabrook liked it. He says so.

He does more. He writes in another place : " That human sacrifice occurs in Voodoo to-day may seem strange and, to many persons, horrible. But only, I think, because they consider it in terms of ' time.' With the time-element removed, and considered in terms of space, religious human sacrifice becomes, in a technical sense, both normal and moral."

I daresay—in fact I know—I am absurdly old-fashioned in my ideas ; but I state almost without hesitation that I do not see eye to eye with Mr. Seabrook over his favourite tipple. With regard to human sacrifices I am a frank reactionary, standing nearer, I should imagine, to the position of the late Mrs. Humphry Ward than to that of Mr. W. B. Seabrook. Nor do I want any of my female relations to go and live in lonely cottages and distil venom or eat beetles and mice. Any girl who insists on going into the heart of Central America and being immolated by a noble, bronze-limbed Indian on a sacrificial stone appears to me to be lacking in refinement and gentility. She may think it gives her harmony and poise, and feel at the moment when the gleaming knife falls a tranquil sweetness and oneness with the whole of universal nature from the beginning of time until now. But I think she is a silly egg.

I suppose it is a kind of return to Nature, comparable to the feeling which inspired the poets of the Lake School. But Wordsworth never lapped blood. I think the circle is too complete.

And if Macaulay's cultured New Zealander ever comes to look at what was London from Westminster, or Charing Cross, or St. Paul's Bridge, I think it would be a great pity if he found a lot of Anglo-Saxon aborigines practising mumbo-jumbo amongst the stones.

JANUARY PICTURES

Edmund Blunden

MORNINGS in January are not often praised ; but here is one which should be. A most celestial light is in it. The sea has given its halcyon blue. Those winged visions must, after all, be explained as gilded clouds. Against those opening infinities of nimble spirits and their abodes, we see the birds of this world in bands, flying as if under the same spell, now dipping, now ascending, now in close throng, and then transformed into a long serpent-line. Against the same budding east, do you not delight to see, like a hieroglyph, the motionless sails of a windmill ? It is not every one now whose window commands that sight. A windmill is one of several rural implements—the plough, the wagon, the harness, the scythe, the flail—which in silence send profound messages. Are they to be called inanimate objects ? Not by me ; they have a life in them, and are historians of man's earliest and latest needs, his earliest and latest friendships :

Ye generous Britons, VENERATE the plough.

The long dead poet of the " Seasons " has expressed my feelings for me exactly : when I see these silent shapes of elemental use and zeal, I become an untutored savage, and could almost enshrine them as idols.

The morning matures into a day of summer weather almost, pleasing us and the many buds and shoots which thrive in our not over-disciplined tenement among the darker, damper greens and lichen yellows. I will not boast of our climate, but, after all, it is something in deep winter to have violets blooming, and now most exquisite for sight and smell ; they bedrop with their white and blue even the bank where we split our wood for a broad hearth. Below the bank the moat fills steadily. In one respect, England is a hard country. Abroad I have seen wretched ditches and water-holes which were populous with fish. But here, how often have I seen a seeming paradise for fishes quite without any ! Perhaps the strata of dead leaves and sticks which hide the bottom of our moat breathe out a poison. We only have, stare as we may, the hint of fishes. That lank drowned tree is dappled with white and green mould ; in shape and markings it is mimicked by the pike. This shorter branch has a part streaked light and dark ; and if it would move one would be deceived into thinking that our moat held perch.

Rain comes on, and our loneliness lasts for a night ; but the return of daylight is once again astonishing. Again the sunlight flows like an elixir over the fluted tiles and the fluttering ivy. This Sunday morning the sound of bell

> Rather like a perfume dwells

about us than a passing tune ; the ringers are faulty in their rhythm, which at a distance helps the notion that the music is a drifting mist. The sun climbs, and the moat's surface, stirred by the moorhens into wavelets as they busy themselves under the root-houses of the banks, or furrowed far as they ply rapidly over, throws the sunlight in a twinkling dance on the old brickwork. Where the mansion stood, the grove is quiet but for the heavy exit of pigeons, taught by past slaughters to trust nobody. This grove is dark with double gloom. The rooks seem to regard it as an ominous landmark; travelling aloft, they rarely pause here or descend, and often start up an excited conversation as they approach. All their enemies cannot get the better of them; and indeed our larger birds, moorhens, pigeons, rooks, barn owls, probably outnumber the little ones.

The memory of a robin entering one's house with familiar readiness was one of the causes of my looking back with sudden intensity to England from the East. We have other pleasures now, which will be added one day to my dreams in exile. There is this friendship, for example, between our little Cockney cat Faust and the half-blind hen, who is indulged, and may feed in the kitchen or where she will indoors. There they doze side by side in a corner of the hen-house by themselves. It is an idyll which at one time seemed improbable. At first Faust regarded Chuck-Chuck with fascination, as the Fool in Shakespeare's play regarded Edgar in disguise for a walking mystery; now and then she put forth a paw for positive assurance that this was an ordinary, material hen. The hen, seeing darkly, took Faust's white paws for something eatable, and pecked at them. The cat still watched with a fixed, scientific eye. Perhaps, had it not been for our own eyes also watching— but Faust knew that. And now you see the mutual sympathy.

Or again, I shall recall how this morning when a window was opened to let in the sunshine, the cockerel was soon on the sill, framed against the bright day; his stately blackness glowed, his comb was a ruby, his challenging posture and his plumage altogether made him a prince of darkness and infernal flames. Meanwhile, a chaffinch went by with a straw in his beak. The illusion of the " swete sesoun " is too much for him. Perhaps he has seen us pretending to play cricket, for in this unfrequented corner we can do so in January without being thought mad. We do so where the Elizabethan gentleman, with the roses on his shoes, had his bowling-green.

> To cure the mind's worst bias, Spleen,
> Some recommend a bowling-green.

Perhaps, in the course of the year, we will renew that tradition here in our unpolished way. I think I can picture the Elizabethans, so playing, so consulting ; for I have seen at Oxford, in the setting of cool grey stonework and twilight flowers, the game at its best. What a magnificence instantly invests the matter when that modern Elizabethan, the Dean of W——, stoops with jack in hand on a summer's evening, and the chaplain (the immortal W. F. S., lamenting Maryland and loving England) judges the situation with serene, paradisal comparisons. And there is R., who is a changed man since he really discovered the passion in the word " sweet wood," and his genius for the green. He has grown into a mystic almost, one who sees the hand that rolls the heavenly orbs, and shares the delight of that propulsive secret.

This is, however, winter's evening. We may do well to step out through the yellowing moonlight, along the empty park, to the " Six Bells," where we know well enough what we shall discover. Twelfth Night will *not* be kept up ; the main music will be the mechanical piano, to the thud of which one or two buxom women will jazz heavily. Christmas revelry will be discussed in the parlour ; it will prove to have been scarcely Falstaffian. " I don't know how ever I did get home that night." " That were at the Agricultural Show. What must Daniel do but get on the bandstand ? They got he off there *somehow*." Our provincial dialect conceals the individual well—as well as the Oxford accent would do. But are we, even here, decadent ? In former times, would these speakers have been drinking bottled beer ? " Old and mild " seems to be going out of favour.

OTHER PEOPLE'S LIVES

Winifred Holtby

WE were walking round the ramparts of St. Malo, waiting for the boat to take us to the other side of the bay. It was a stormy summer evening, and because of the premature gloom the townspeople had lit their lamps early, without drawing their curtains. From our vantage point, high on the broad stone walls, we could look straight into bedrooms and living-rooms that leapt to dramatic light out of the steep grey houses. Here sat fathers of families, bending purposefully over the red-checked tablecloth, dipping their rich moustaches into steaming *bouillon*, while their offspring, with the liberty common to most French children, clustered confidently around, awaiting their turn, and munching indigestible - looking chunks of bread. We saw mothers putting babies into their cradles, peeling onions, folding clothes, and arguing, arms akimbo, with their husbands. In one bourgeois parlour, crammed with knick-nacks, a family in deep mourning sat stiffly, obviously receiving a state call. In another, a man and girl danced dreamily to the raucous music of a cheap gramophone. Her auburn head nestled against his blue pullover. Their bodies, locked together, swayed in ecstatic union ; they were utterly oblivious of their ugly little room, of the gusts of rain driving from time to time against their window, and of us, watching shamelessly from the ramparts.

"Other people's lives," sighed my companion, "are always so exciting."

I laughed at her romantic mood, although I shared it. She had not done so badly herself. She had been married, divorced, shipwrecked, had held various unusual and interesting jobs, published a book or two, travelled up remote rivers in a canoe, alone among strange men, had seen the Northern Lights, been involved in lawsuits, given evidence in a *cause célèbre*—any one would think that she had lived through adequately varied and dramatic experiences. Not at all. She leaned over the damp stone, gazing, absorbed, into the cluttered room where a Breton fishmonger's wife was telling a neighbour of the iniquitous price she paid for her husband's underpants (at least, that was what the scene suggested to our fascinated eyes), and she was sighing, "Other people's lives are *so* exciting."

Of course, she was right. They are; especially the brief, dramatic glimpses that one has of them, seen through a lighted window, or from a passing train, or deduced from a snatch of conversation overheard on a bus.

Windows particularly. I know of few cheaper and more satisfying entertainments than that of walking along Sloane Street, or down Eaton Square, just before dinner in the evening, when all the basement windows are lighted and few of the curtains drawn. There one can see butlers preening themselves before the looking-glass, straightening their ties, smoothing the scanty hair over their shining heads—a glorious spectacle, a sight for the gods, indeed. I have seen butlers scolding housemaids. I have seen one of these godlike persons teaching an under parlour-maid, presumably, how to pass the peas. Best of all, I have seen a butler, the boots, and two maidservants, enjoying with great solemnity a game of Bridge. How remote, how splendid seem the lives of butlers, seen through the basement windows of Eaton Square ! Like strange, majestic fish floating in their lighted tanks in the Aquarium at the Zoo. Indeed, I always feel that part of the fascination of the Aquarium lies in the sense which it gives us of intrusion into the private lives of plaice and whiting.

But lives observed from the train in foreign countries are even more stimulating. I have watched with passionate eagerness the domestic amenities of Italian peasants, brown-faced and talkative, unrolling from bundles long loaves, slices of cold fried meat, and bottles of red wine, as they sat contentedly on the platforms of little stations, waiting without impatience for the local train. There were two girls with a goat in the hard-bitten, littered, dried-up courtyard of an Apennine farm ; at the sudden whistle of a young man they both turned simultaneously : he came through the broken gate, his teeth gleaming, his arms outstretched, towards—which ? The train snatched us away before we knew.

It is this fragmentary, precarious glimpse caught by the traveller, this brief, limited, perfect picture seen through the lighted window, that gives their dramatic intensity to these peep-shows. I shall never know what punishment was meted out to the black baby whom I saw once from a car in the Northern Transvaal, caught by a handsome Negro woman red-handed, in the act of sticking thorns through a grand orange blanket stretched airing on the bush. I shall never know what became of the Hungarian student who, at three o'clock in the morning, in a Budapest café, described how he and his companions were drilling nightly outside an old country house, preparing themselves for the day when they would drive the wicked Roumanians out of Transylvania. I shall never know what happened to the tired-looking, pretty English woman, rowed across to our ship from Ascension Island by a rather bored and weary husband, when we called there in 1926. She wanted to buy face creams and powders in our barber's shop. She wore the clothes that had been very fashionable three years before. She and her husband were obviously worn out by each other's company in that small, hot, isolated, quarrelsome little community, on a barren island where there is so little to do for a young bride who is brought there by a junior officer of the Eastern Telegraph Company.

We shall never know. Our contact is like reading one instalment of a serial story, of which we cannot procure the beginning nor the end. But having seen one incident, we hunger for more. It is strange ; so it must be dramatic. It is different ; so it must be better.

There is a rather touching humility in this widespread human trait. It is so hard for us to think of ourselves as the centre of any picture.

I remember that when I was at school I was frequently consumed by envy and admiration for a little clique of athletic and handsome girls whom I and my more studious friends called " Them." " They " seemed to be cocks in every roost ; " They " seemed to us to be glamorous and splendid ; their homes were large halls and " county " places ; they hunted ; they got into tennis teams and hockey elevens ; they knew how to keep their hair tidy ; and one of them actually lived abroad in Ostende. Not long ago I met one of " Them," now a married woman with a little boy who writes fairy stories. I told her of my former envious admiration. " Oh, but how funny ! " she cried. " We used to call you and your friends ' Them.' You see, you always got the big parts in the plays ; you wrote in the school magazine ; you made up the songs for the Guide concerts. We were nowhere beside you and your lot."

So there we were, each profoundly convinced that the others had the exciting lives. But that illusion is by no means confined to schoolgirls. A few weeks ago I went with a party to the Savoy Grill, and we sat at a table in the big window watching the crowds coming out of the theatre across the courtyard. " Oh, *do* look at that girl from the upper circle waiting for her young man ! " we cried. " Oh, he's not her young man. He must be her father." " It's not her father. Look at the way he takes her arm. He's an old lover, and he's trying to make her marry him. . . ." " No, he's an uncle. Here comes Auntie ! " " What fun this is. I'm so glad we got a table in the window. Here one can sit and really see life." Yet, suddenly, I remembered the number of times when I had come out of the upper circle or pit at the Savoy Theatre, and gazed across into the lighted windows of the grill room at the ladies and gentlemen in evening dress, and thought, "How glad I am that we came to this theatre. Here I can see straight into the Savoy Hotel. Those are the really rich, eating smoked salmon. This," I had thought, "is what I call seeing life."

When we see life in this way, it is the homely and domestic details which give us the thrill of authenticity. The only time I ever shook hands with a queen, I noticed that one button had come off her white kid glove. Now the pleasure given by that observation was nothing to do with the irreverent iconoclastic appetite for any debunking of royalty. I did not in the least want to see royalty debunked. I like my queens to be queenly. But I could not help being pleased because I had seen something so homely and intimate about her. Buttons coming off gloves at the last moment—or, indeed, even after the last moment, when it is already too late to do anything about it—was an experience that I could understand. I could imagine Her Majesty saying: "Dear, dear!" or "Tut, tut," or "Drat the thing!" or whatever queens do say; and screwing the glove round to wonder if it showed.

This mingling of the familiar and the strange is what invests with enchantment those glimpses we steal into other people's lives. "Look, in Finland they sit round stoves—not open fires. But they drink tea as well as coffee, and look,

that woman is darning her daughter's sock."
" Just fancy, that black Kikuyu girl is dressing
for a ball. Her beads aren't the right size.
She's disappointed. Just like me, when my shoes
were the wrong shade for the Cricket Dance."
" Look, that Red Indian has broken the line of
his fishing rod. And he'd told his wife he was
going to bring home the supper. And she nags
like anything. Aren't they like Auntie Maud
and Uncle Arthur ? "

The diversity of individual experience and the
unity of human nature, those are the two reiterated
notes of the travellers' tale. To see life is to see
lives which might be ours, and yet which are
different.

Thus to-day do some yearn for South Sea
Islands, and some for Soviet Russia ; in Moscow
they sing songs of " Chicago ! City Built upon a
Screw." In Chicago there are rum-runners and
hi-jackers who sigh for Italian vineyards, and
stone-built houses with onions drying under the
open rafters, and quiet-eyed cattle dragging the
heavy wagons past the open door. Townspeople
dream of country lanes and moonlit daisies
starring the sleeping meadow ; country people
sigh for Piccadilly Circus, and listen with envious
ears to the trains roaring down to London through
the night.

This is the great romantic urge of society,
driving it towards a future about which the only
quality predictable is that it will not be precisely
like the past. We are all in love with the lives
that are not our lives, the homes that are not our
homes, even, many of us, with the times that are
not our times. We all want something, and will

not be happy till we get it, and shan't be happy
then, for we shall still want something else.
Glory is always waiting just beyond the garden
in somebody else's home, not ours; for some
other golden and glowing person, not ourselves.
Some of us do nothing about it, being wistful
romantics who love to hug the thought of perfection lying—somewhere. Others are stirred to
ambition, like the seekers of power in Hobbes's
Leviathan for whom "felicity is a continual
progresse of the desire from one object to another,
the attaining of the former being still but the way
to the latter . . . and there shall be no content-
ment but proceeding."

RADIO DRAMA

Val Gielgud

THERE are few subjects connected with broadcasting that have caused so much in the way of
controversy as the broadcasting of plays. This
may be partly due to the fact that the immediate
reaction of the ordinary listener—to whom the
word " play " has very definite implications,
including scenery, limelights, and good-looking
actors or actresses—is that to attempt to broadcast drama is either impossible or ridiculous, and
quite probably both.

Alternatively, few programme items have re-
ceived quite so much publicity, both desirable
and undesirable, as the broadcast play, owing to
the rather peculiar machinery of the medium.
The Dramatic Control Panel and the technique of
the multiple studio method—not to mention the
singular contents of the famous Effects Studio
with its tin baths, its drums, its match boxes that
represent wrecks, and its potatoes that represent
avalanches—have been an irresistible temptation
to writers on the look-out for something slightly
unusual in the way of subject. Consequently,
for a long time the very possibility of broadcasting
plays was by some people considered a dubious
one, while others read that what sounded like

an enormously complicated mechanism was employed in the process of such productions.

It would be foolish to deny that absence of visuality is a handicap which it is difficult to overcome by any degree of the ingenuity or elaboration of special technique. People are used to " seeing plays," and it is not easy to induce people who are used to doing anything to make the necessary effort to do something else which is, nevertheless, called the same thing. It is true that an audience, by its original meaning, implies people who listen rather than people who see, but it is a far cry nowadays from that age of the drama in which the spoken word and the speaking of that word were by far the most important part of its presentation. The broadcast play, therefore, has not only to contend with maintaining the interest of the people who listen to it, but it has, in the first place, to persuade potential listeners that if they listen at all they will hear something worth while. The original notion that, by putting a few microphones about a stage and telling the actors to curtail their normal " business," it is possible to reproduce faintly and haltingly a normal stage representation of a play is, fortunately, as dead as the dodo —most fortunately, because as long as the notion persisted, there was no chance of radio drama ever being anything else but a *pis aller* of the most banal description ; most fortunately, too, because professional broadcasters, having been driven to the discovery of a special technique of the presentation of plays, have realized that the adoption and use of such special presentation in the handling of nearly all broadcast programme items will add something like fifty per cent. in efficiency and entertainment value to those items.

While it can hardly be claimed that the majority of the problems of producing plays on the air have been successfully solved, it is not unreasonable to claim a very considerable advance both in the technique of production and in the content of plays broadcast during the last few years. Such progress has been largely due to two things—to the increasing professional competence of producers, and to the establishment of the broadcast play as a professionally recognized medium of dramatic representation, however humble. The time has gone by when the producer of broadcast plays was regarded as an amiable amateur, unprofitably employed, wasting time, money, and talent on barren experiments dispatched into an unresponsive void ; a time when actors regarded broadcasting engagements in a light far from sympathetic ; a time when the Effects Studio was the favourite joke of the wireless press. It is doubtful if the average man or woman who is in the habit of going to the theatre is kept away by the alternative of being offered a radio play, but radio drama has never for a moment entered into competition with the theatre, and it is devoutly hoped that it never will. If anything, it is something of a free advertising agent of the theatre by tending to make the average listener dramatically minded to the stage at which he or she will go for himself and see a play, if circumstances of space and economics are favourable. But there is a considerable amount of evidence that, among those listeners who are so situated that a theatre is not a daily or weekly feature of their lives, the radio play is one of the most hotly discussed of programme items. It has violent assailants, and fierce defenders, and by foreign broadcasting authorities it is generally recognized that under the British system of production it achieves its best results. That this is so is probably due to the fact that the B.B.C. was the first broadcasting organization to realize the enormous advantages of the Dramatic Control Panel and the technique of multiple studios. This technique enables the producer, while separating the ingredients of his production into various studios of varying acoustic values, at the same time to control the different output of all these studios with his own hand, and maintain a proper perspective with regard to the whole production by rehearsing from the distance of several floors away. After the first two or three rehearsals the producer's contact with his cast is one of voice alone. While to some extent this theory has been adopted by some of the more up-to-date Continental radio producers, most of them are loath to part with that immediate personal control of their actors which the distant Dramatic Control Panel implies. The result is that they are liable to forget that their actors make up only one ingredient of a play in which sound sequences and music may easily be of equal or even greater value. The result is that proper aural perspective is often neither achieved nor maintained.

It may be that the broadcast play will be of all artistic mediums the most short lived. The shadow of television is rapidly lengthening on the wall, and few prophets will be hardy enough to maintain—with the example of the cinema before their eyes—that, once sight has come to supplement sound, however dimly, listeners will ever be content again with sound alone. But even if that is so, there may be found among the records of the earlier years of broadcasting a small niche for the broadcast play, which, if it has done nothing else, has at least succeeded in a task that baffled both the theatre and the schools : radio drama has brought Shakespeare to life in every town and village in these islands.

WASHING DAY

Rosalind Vallance

WHEN I got up this morning it was blowing and clouding, and shining and trying to rain, and doing all four at once, and then stopping to get its breath and doing it again harder than ever; so when the others said, "Let's go bathing," I had a vision of a sea full of wild white horses (that's nice), very cold ones (that's nasty), and nowhere to undress where things didn't flap, and sand blowing into your eyes, and rain getting into the chocolate, so I said I'd got toothache and had better stay at home in the Mill-house. And I got my writing things and began to settle, and the others went off. And then the sun came out, so I thought I'd have a washing day. When you've been on holiday for three weeks the handkerchief-and-stocking question gets a bit 'bothering.' So I collected some, and a piece of soap, and pen and paper, and came up-stream. And here I am; and I've done the washing, and the sun's still shining, and I'm very happy.

Do you know how to have a washing day in a mountain stream? Well, first you look among your collection of shoes for the wettest pair, for you know they'll be worse by the end of the morning, and you mustn't waste half-dried ones, for you'll want those to be grand with in the evening in the village. So you struggle into the wet ones, and you slush up the lane, which the night rain has turned into an imitation marsh.

You disturb the miller's chickens in their morning gossip at the well, and they all go scuttering before you like a lot of flustered old ladies, and squeeze through the fence and start getting lost on the mountain-side ; so of course you have to collect them, and push them back, squawking and terrified, over the fence again. You stop to peer for a moment into the dark rush and swirl of water in the willowy pool below the mill, and to call out " Good-morning " to the floury old man himself.

He's the whitest thing you ever saw, and he even has a long white beard to match. He can't hear what you say, because of the gr— gr— of the great stone wheels and the everlasting slush and rumble of the water, but he smiles benevolently. You know he is smiling by the twinkle in his old brown eyes. Often they look dull ; you feel he isn't seeing much through them : perhaps he is looking inward at the past, but he always brightens if you ask him anything about the mill. His sister, who is old, too, tells us that he feels very sadly in the days when there's no one bringing grist. " There's new ways of doing things now," she says, " Ess," and sighs such a pathetic little old sigh. But this morning we heard a farmer's cart rumble up the lane, and it didn't go on up to the moor, but turned round by the deserted pig-sties into the mill yard. And soon we heard the wheels thundering round. So the old man is happy to-day, and I left him smiling and humming to himself. His sister says he can sing like a robin, though he is over eighty ; and I don't wonder, for I hadn't been eighty *minutes* here before I felt song beginning to well up—even in me ; and he is Welsh, and has had eighty years of robins and rivers to teach him music.

What about the washing ? All in good time ; and, if not, it doesn't matter : one thing here is quite as good as another—generally better !

Well, I left the miller standing in his cobwebby old place (and even the cobwebs are white, and so are the long fingers of ivy and bramble that have pushed in through the cracks). I left him, and walked over the glistening grass to the Picnic Place.

The Picnic Place is the loveliest spot in Wales. But it was not made for a washing-day morning. Oh no. You couldn't possibly do anything so workish there. The Picnic Place is for sunny afternoons, a book, and tea to follow very soon. You can tell tales in the Picnic Place, or lie on your back half asleep and watch the clouds sailing like galleons, or anything else you fancy, over the mountain-tops.

Or, contrariwise, you can lie on your tummy and throw sticks and orange-boats and paper bags into the stream, and watch them race to their doom in the deep mill-pool ; or you can dam up a corner of the stream and make a pond, big enough, and small enough, for sailing your penny boat without fear of wreckage.

For the Picnic Place is a little green lawn beside the river. There are rocks and bracken

behind to keep the wind off, and " back-centre,"
as they say in plays, is the most perfect old
hawthorn tree ; a little gnarled and bent—really
stagey. We *feel* stagey whenever we come to the
Picnic Place, and always put on our brightest
frocks and pullovers. We should twine flowers
in our hair if there were any of the twiny kind
here, but there aren't at present, only blackberry,
which pricks, and heather, which is too " bitty,"
so we don't.

Besides, they'd be sure to fall out the minute
we began to play stepping-stones ; they would
fall into the water and be swirled away, faster
and faster, in and out among the grey stones,
down to the dangerous mill-race ; or they'd be
marooned in one of the clear, deep little pools,
and pretend to be water-lilies, and we'd never
have the heart to fish them out again. So we
don't twine flowers in our hair, though we should
so much like to.

You can see now why the Picnic Place would
never do for a wash-house. You must paddle
up-stream to find one. You have stopped bothering about the feel of water squelching over your
toes, making funny little gugglings inside your
shoes, for you know that in two minutes you
won't even pretend to use the stepping-stones,
but you'll take the salmon-fisher's way of getting
along. It's a bit cold, but you soon get used to
that, and the water is so soft and silky you know
it will heal all the blisters and cuts left over from
yesterday's walk on the mountains. It's so
delicious, plunging from one silky swirl to the
next little stony shallow, scrambling over a big
rock and under an overhanging branch, that,

when at last you find the wash-house, you've almost forgotten you were looking for it.

But there it is, a little side-water that part of the river made for itself one hot day when it was too lazy to keep rushing along with the main stream.

There is everything here the heart of washer-woman can desire : a deep, clear tank for the first wash, with just a small current flowing through, enough to keep it fresh and sweet, but not enough to snatch the clothes out of your hands ; a great flat rock for a scrubbing-board, and a little water-fall just below for rinsing. And the hankies can have a final boil in the little whirlpool the water-fall makes.

But the exciting part is getting the things dry. You try the flat stones in mid-stream ; they are warm and dry. But a gust of wind comes, and when you come back with a hanky you have chased from rock to rock, the stockings have flown away, one into the whirlpool, and one on to the muddy bank. So you give up the flat stone and try the jagged ones. They hold on a little longer, but there's still an unsafe feeling about them. You can't lie on the grass and turn your back on them comfortably. No, rocks won't do. And bracken swallows the clothes, and haw-thorn tears them, and the willow casts them treacherously back into the stream. But the aspen tree is just right. She holds them gently but surely in her arms, and swings them to and fro among her own grey leaves over the stream.

" Hush, my darlings ; dry yourselves, my darlings," says the tree.

She's looking after them for me now, while I write.